Take a Bite of Eternal Life

Volume I

BY MICHAEL F. BLUME

Take a Bite of Eternal Life
Volume I

By Michael F. Blume

Copyright ©2007 Michael F. Blume

First Printing 2007

Cover Design by Michael F. Blume

Printed in China

For additional copies see:
THAT I MAY KNOW HIM
Website Ministry of Michael F. Blume
www.mikeblume.com

Garden City Publications

Winnipeg, Manitoba

To
Iris

TABLE OF CONTENTS

v

ACKNOWLEDGEMENTS

I thank my uncle, and mentor of my mentors, William Bustard, who has gone on to be with the Lord. I will never forget the day you told me you heard from the Lord about the nature of my ministry, and yet could not relate it to me since you felt the Lord should confirm it, first. Then, weeks later, while giving my morning devotions presentation in our Bible School, I felt to "teach," although I was only a student. You wept and praised the Lord as I ministered, and later told me that day this is what the Lord showed you that I would be doing for Him. Your urge for the students to ever reach out and lean upon God's Spirit opened up an avenue of revelation to my soul in studying God's Word for which I am eternally grateful. I wish you were still with us down here.

I also wish to give many thanks to Jamen Nicholson for his tremendous ministry and gift of giving for the work of the Lord. Your revelation is truly genuine and God-sent for this hour in God's Kingdom.

AUTHOR'S PREFACE

In every age there are people who hunger for all God has to offer for both now and afterwards in glory. There are those who long to follow Him into every depth into which He would lead them. Something grips their hearts when they read accounts of the cries of Moses and Paul to truly "know" God. It catches their spirits every time they read intimate terminology in the bible associating believers with their God, such as "face to face." And what is even more wonderful is that God's seven *eyes*, that are sent forth to search the entire world, locate every soul who has this drive within them, and He hunts them down!

God has been peeling away the veil from the hearts of Christians, who forever want to venture further into truths, and experience all they can experience today and forever, while knowing that God's realm of experience is endless! What a time to be serving God!

You and I are on the cutting edge of time. Think of it! Our entire generation is the latest thing on planet Earth. God is working in such a way as to complement that fact. He so desperately desires that we have all the joy and fulfillment of Life that He can possibly give us. After two thousand years of Church history, it is high time God's people enter into the fullness of all our salvation can provide us in the here and now.

From Genesis to Revelation, the panoramic vista of God's astounding plan of the ages unfolds before our spirits as we study with hearts hungry for truth. There are depths in God's Word that are presently being excavated from the holy writ, causing His people to delve into the riches of the fullness of Christ, and to know our Lord in a far greater manner than anyone has ever imagined, before we even arrive in Heaven! We are the closest to Christ's return than anybody has ever been, and things are certain to be the most exciting right now. And it can only get better!

It is God's desire to unfold the entire scope of the written revelation to His church and have us learn how to enjoy all that Christ died on the cross for us to enjoy. So many have relegated all wonder and blessing into their past as they look back at the cross or to revivals of the past. People also tend to look to our future in Heaven. But the Lord has so much wondrous victory and peace for us in this present world of which most have never been made aware. He placed the Garden of Eden *in this Earth*.

God had a plan for humanity when He created man from the dust of the earth. What was it? Try to imagine what God's purpose for Adam was had Adam never sinned. And keep in mind that death only came to man due to sin (Romans 5:12), which tells us that Adam was meant to live forever in a physical body in a physical world. Dying and going to Heaven was an unknown thing for man's original purpose. We were never meant to die. Whatever it was meant to be, it is restored in the church! This is not to say there is no Heaven, as such, in which we will experience wonders we could not begin to imagine. But for some reason we have been made to think God has abandoned this physical plain for some reason since Adam's fall. This is simply not true.

All the wonderful parallels we find in the work of God in the church compared to the Garden of Eden tell us God never abandoned His will for mankind in this earth that He first planned for Adam. Even the book of Revelation shows the New Jerusalem descending *to the Earth* with the tree of Life, last seen in the Garden, within its midst. Nothing in the Bible indicates that anything will change as to what God purposed for humanity in the Garden of Eden. We are meant to understand that every aspect of the Garden is involved in our restoration participation with God in His Kingdom.

Jesus told us to pray for His will to be done in earth as it is in heaven. To what extent is His will done in heaven?

Salvation literally means deliverance. Adam threw us all into sin, and it is that state from which we are delivered. This can only mean a restoration to that state and position from which Adam fell. Jesus is even called the last man Adam! Was only part of what Adam lost that which is restored in salvation? I think not.

Man was intended to have almost unbelievable blessings *in this life*, and dominion over every facet of life. Unfortunately, man fell from fellowship with God and lost that opportunity. But that plan was not lost forever, to leave us waiting in this world until He takes us Home to Glory before we can enjoy what He first planned for life on Earth.

Jesus said, "The Kingdom is in you." It will never come with observation, for it is an invisible Kingdom, and we have been born into it, of the water and of the Spirit. It is spiritual dominion, righteousness, peace and joy in the Holy Spirit. Before this eon is complete, God will have raised up a church with the power and dominion and glory He initially intended for Adam and Eve. His Spirit so wants to open up the first few chapters of Genesis to us all, and to return us, in faith, to that status of power in His Kingdom, for therein lay the very basics of the entire remainder of the Bible, and the extent of power and Life we can enjoy today as believers. From that foundational understanding, we will see His complete will fulfilled throughout the holy writ. In other words, the first few chapters of Genesis set the pace for the complete desired work of God in our lives regarding our time in this present world, and in the world to come. They are literally packed full of truths that we must come to understand in order to properly put into place all the seemingly mysterious passages elsewhere in the Book. All of this will fulfill the longing desire in both our hearts and that of the Lord's.

This is the first volume of a planned two volume set. Let us begin by spanning the entire Bible, concentrating especially upon the uncanny parallels between the first book Genesis, (specifically its first few chapters) and the last book, Revelation, and concentrating upon the wondrous typology associated with this overall concept.

Michael F. Blume
May 2006

1

BITE INTO ETERNAL LIFE

The entire account of creation, including the very first human couple, Adam and Eve, emphasizes the focal point of *the Tree of Life*. God obviously intended for us to grasp a certain truth regarding this Tree. This concept never departs from Scripture.

The second chapter of Genesis recounts God's placement of man into the Garden in order to dress and keep it. This reveals that the Garden was intended to expand and increase on the earth! Try to imagine a world overridden by a veritable Garden of Eden! That's exactly what God intended Adam to initiate. The Lord's goal was to see the Garden spread across and encompass the entire world. Something about all of this that comes to us in the form of a foreboding warning, though, is God's Word to Adam to keep, or *protect*, that Garden in the process. But, protect it from what?

At the outset of the man's life in the Garden, God said Adam could eat the fruit from any of the trees in the Garden, including the Tree of Life. He was simply not to eat of the fruit from the Tree of the Knowledge of Good and Evil. If you notice carefully, this reference to the Tree of Life *is the first word mentioned* in relation to Adam's life in the Garden,

1

and it's also *the last detailed reference from that period.* At the end of Adam's life in the Garden, God said He had to remove man lest he take of *the fruit of life,* eat and live forever. This Tree is clearly an important aspect in the unfolding story of mankind. God wants us to keep it in mind.

We are all familiar with the story's end, when the woman, whom God created for the man, was tempted by Satan to take fruit from the very tree that was forbidden. She fell to the temptation, influenced her husband, and he also ate. We recognize this as the first sin – disobedience – in the recorded history of mankind.

As a result, God cursed the ground for man's sake, and then cursed the woman as well as the serpent that tempted her. He proceeded to drive the people from the Garden for the distinct purpose of disallowing them to eat from the Tree of Life. Notice this: It was originally God's will for them to eat of the Tree of Life – but after man sinned, it wasn't. Why?

When God thrust the man and his wife out of the Garden, He indicated that Adam must be separated from the Tree of Life lest he eat of it and live forever.

To understand this, we must consider that the Garden was a holy place absent of sinful elements. In casting man from the Garden, God averted the possibility of an evil infection plaguing mankind *permanently.* You see, after his sin, man was required *to die* in order for recovery from sin to be possible. Otherwise, with sin in his life and no possibility of death, Adam would be rendered incapable of the potential for redemption. All this can be understood when considering that

2

Christ was planned to come millennia later and *die* for mankind, in man's place, and thereby redeem those who would believe and obey this Gospel. The way in which this redemption would work is based upon the principle of Atonement. The sacrificial death counts as the death of the offerer of the sacrifice. It thereby pays the death penalty that was sentenced upon the offerer by proxy, or substitution. If we could not die, there could be no substitute, or vicarious, sacrifice.

Before Adam sinned, God had a plan for him in this world – a plan that was without death, for death only came into this world by sin. Without sin, there would not have been any form of death (Romans 5:12). We might not be able to comprehend such a world without death, but we must ever remember God's awesome plan for this world and humanity! Let's not limit God's abilities by surveying the present state of things and determining what God can do based upon what we see in the world today.

There are details about the coming of Jesus Christ that reveal how the overall pattern of God's original purpose for Adam remained in God's plan. Jesus was called the "last man Adam". The Church can be considered his "Eve," who was made from his flesh and bone, as the original Eve was made from Adam's flesh and bones (Ephesians 5:30-32). Adam's predicament of sin would only be resolved by way of the remedy of sacrifice, and Jesus would come to be that very sacrifice. And by the term "remedy" we mean that God would fully restore everything lost in the Garden, and recommence with the initial plan for mankind that Adam was intended to experience.

3

Since Adam became prey to death as a result of his sin, *sacrificial death* would be the key for his salvation. It would pay the price for sin and settle the problem. Had man become immortal by eating of the fruit of Life, he could not have been rescued by a sacrificial death, the only salvation from sin by the principle of *Atonement*.

Let me explain. Leviticus 1:4 informs us that an Atonement sacrifice would be accepted *for*, or *"as"*, the one offering the sacrifice, in order to make atonement for him. Atonement is literally the coming together of two separated people – at-*one*-ment. God and man were separated due to man's sin. Through this payment for sin, they once again became "at one" in beautiful fellowship again, or *atoned*. The sacrifice would be *accepted for him*, or, accepted *as him,* as if he actually died, himself.

TWO FORBIDDEN FRUIT, NOT JUST ONE

The fruit of Life contained the power to cause man to live forever! So, with sin dwelling in man's flesh, the story of Adam's time in the Garden ends with two fruit, instead of one, labeled as strictly forbidden to man by God.

Keep in mind that the only reason Adam was initially allowed to eat of the fruit of Life, and then forbidden to eat it, was obviously due to the difference of initially not possessing sin, and then later winding up with sin in his flesh. Therefore, even today, sin is the only thing in man's way that keeps him from walking to the Tree of Life and eating its fruit!

Yes, the Tree of Life is still God's plan for mankind even today! It is not so much a physical tree with natural fruit that He desires for our sakes now, but the same *concept* and the same *pattern* has never changed since Adam's day. God's plan was not trashed due to some oversight God experienced as though He did not expect Satan to thwart His will for humanity. Before creation began, the Lord *foreknew* the tragedy that would occur after creation, and the Lamb was already slain from the foundation of the world in the sense that He was preplanned to do so.

CHERUBIMIC BARRIER

But Adam did sin, and was driven outside the Garden and away from that Tree due to his sin. Ever since that dreadful day, mankind has been born and has lived outside the Garden, spiritually speaking.

A very notable point is mentioned in conjunction with Adam's expulsion from the Garden. *A bladed and creatured barrier* blocked Adam's way to the tree of Life was. God placed a flaming sword that turned in every direction, along with creatures He called Cherubims, to keep Adam from the Tree of Life (Genesis 3:24).

Imagine Adam standing *outside* the Garden and gazing at its entrance. If he could only pass those Cherubims and that flaming sword, he could walk to the tree of life, pluck the fruit of life from its branch and give to his wife! Both of them could eat that fruit and live forever! But no. Instead, the woman walked up to the forbidden tree, plucked its fruit, and then gave to her husband. They both ate and spiritually died, just as God forewarned. These strange barriers then became the keepers of the way to the Tree of Life, barring out the *former keepers* of the beautiful Garden.

These cherubims were stationed at the entrance to keep, or protect, the way of the tree of life. But do not be mistaken! The Tree, itself, did not require protection. Adam required it! Should Adam be freely given access to the Tree of Life, with sin still residing in him, he would surely doom himself forever. Once again, we must stress this point: Without the ability to die, humanity would not have the potential to *identify* with the Lord in His then-future death for them, in order to thereby save us all from sin. One must have the potential to die in order for Christ to die for, and save one from, sin. There must be that "communion", or *mutual participation*, involved in the concept of the death of the Cross for man's salvation. Today we are crucified *with Christ*, when we are saved from sin.

Imagine a man who is unable to die, and thereby unable *to be saved* through the death of the cross!

A STRANGE REACTION TO SIN

The first man and woman experienced a most strange reaction after they ate the forbidden fruit. This reaction informs us that the Tree of the Knowledge of Good and Evil was unlike anything we might think about common fruit. When they ate this fruit...

> ...*the eyes of them both were opened, and they knew that they were naked; and they sewed fig leaves together, and made themselves aprons. Genesis 3:7.*

BITE INTO ETERNAL LIFE

Formerly it was said of them...

And they were both naked, the man and his wife, and were not ashamed. Genesis 2:25

Obviously, the eating of the fruit inspired shame for their nakedness, and moved them to physically cover themselves after eating it. Eating the fruit accomplished something very spiritual within the man and woman. Ordinary fruit does not do that! Rest assured -- the forbidden fruit was definitely not an apple!

If the forbidden fruit caused them to experience that kind of reaction, what might they have experienced had they eaten the fruit of Life? We already know it would have caused them to live forever due to God's words about His need to cast them from the Garden, but it seems there would have been more to it than just that. The forbidden fruit did something to their understanding. Even Satan told the woman that the forbidden fruit would make her as "wise as God". There was some truth to his words, although he obviously twisted the true understanding. Could the eating of the fruit of Life would have caused them to experience something in their faculty of knowledge, also? Both the forbidden fruit and the eternal fruit of Life were no ordinary fruit, indeed!

Well, Adam and Eve never did get a chance to eat of the fruit of Life, so we cannot look to their story for the answer. However, the rest of the pages of the Bible do reveal what would have happened, albeit indirectly, if we read them with the Garden pattern of the will of God in mind.

TAKE A BITE OF ETERNAL LIFE

God still desires us to possess Eternal Life! We know that from the Gospel, for it concentrates upon the reference to Life above everything else, just as the Garden account first did.

We will find God's Word reveals that Cherubims and a flaming sword *still keep the way to the Tree of Life*. Spiritually speaking, God wants us to pass the Cherubimic barrier, walk to the Tree of Life, pluck its fruit, eat and give that wonderful fruit to others.

Every word within the Bible has a determined purpose. Don't miss a syllable! With that in mind, consider the picture of the woman plucking the fruit and giving it to someone else, namely her husband. It is written in that manner for a good reason. The *pattern* of *taking fruit* and *giving it to another* is a very major thought in God's Word.

Look at mankind's opportunity for salvation from the standpoint of the picture of Adam's gaze at the Garden's entrance from the outside, and try to imagine a resolution for salvation outside the understanding of the work of the cross. Adam knew nothing about the cross to come. I can imagine Adam thinking, "If I could only pass those Cherubims, walk to the tree of life and pluck its fruit, could I not give eternal life to the rest of humanity?" The answer is "no". Everyone is born in sin. It's not as easy simple as someone simply walking into the Garden to obtain the fruit of Life, given the opportunity. Adam's single act caused us all to become *sinners* before we were even born (Romans 5:19), and such unholy people cannot enter this most holy place. That was the reason Adam was forbidden from going to the Tree of Life to live forever after he sinned.

8

We did not have to commit one single act of sin in order to be called "sinners", since Adam's act was the sole cause. Due to that sin, none of us can, in effect, pass those Cherubims and that sword to be able to approach the tree, pluck its fruit and give to the rest of us! Abel and Cain were born, and did not commit the sin of eating the forbidden fruit that their parents committed. But still, they could not enter the Garden either! That is precisely the case for every human being born since. What a plight mankind was put in! And the devil delighted in it... but it would not be long before he realized something was afoot, and that God had not abandoned the thought of the original plan!

A GLIMMER OF HOPE TO COME

With man then cast out of the Garden and away from fellowship with God, things looked pretty grim. However, a glimmer of hope came forward much later in time. Moses arrived on the scene to lead Israel out of their bondage in Egypt, and was told about something that was directly connected to the predicament of man's expulsion from the Garden. God instructed him to build a Tabernacle – a holy and portable sanctuary that could be transported across the wilderness on their way to the Promised Land. Wherever they stopped and set up camp in the wilderness, the Tabernacle was erected. This would be their place of worship – their sanctuary.

Curtains and a veil were to be constructed and hung around the Tabernacle's most vital compartment amongst all the other Tabernacle trappings and furniture as described in the book of Exodus. These curtains and veil were to be embroidered with *Cherubims* (Exodus 26:1, 31).

TAKE A BITE OF ETERNAL LIFE

Ah... Where did we read about them before?

The curtains and veil were embroidered with the likeness of the very same creatures that barred Adam from the Tree of Life! Cherubims! God told Moses to hang them up in the Tabernacle, with the veil specifically placed over the entrance to a room that was called the Most Holy Place. It would bar people from that Holiest chamber.

> *And thou shalt hang up the veil under the taches, that thou mayest bring in thither within the veil the ark of the testimony: and the veil shall divide unto you between the holy place and the most holy. Exodus 26:33*

Here we see precisely the same picture as with the Cherubims of the Garden. This *cherubim-embroidered* veil barred man from a very holy place just as Cherubims blocked Adam from the Tree of Life! Truly, God was still thinking about the Garden of Eden when He instructed Moses to build the Tabernacle! This same basic layout was also used later in the Temple built by Solomon.

Back in Genesis Chapter 3, God placed the Cherubims at *the east* of the Garden. And, remarkably, the veiled entrance to the Holiest place of the Tabernacle was an entrance that also stood on the *east side of the room*. One would enter the outer court that stood at the east of the whole complex, and walk westward towards the veil. The most holy place stood beyond that veil. It was in this chamber that the most important and significant item was situated – the Ark of the Covenant (Exodus 26:33).

10

BITE INTO ETERNAL LIFE

Like the Tree of Life situated past the barrier of Cherubims and flaming sword, something about proceeding towards that Ark portrayed the then-future work of Jesus Christ. He would come and obtain eternal life for us, like picking fruit from the Tree of Life. He would proceed to give it to mankind, and give us all *a bite of Eternal Life*.

2

PASSING BY
THE CHERUBIMS

Only one man was allowed to pass the veil on only one day a year, called the Day of Atonement. This man was called the High Priest. His entire ceremony during that day stands as a divine pattern for us! He would pass beyond the veil that was embroidered with Cherubims, into the most holy compartment of the Tabernacle. There, he would sprinkle blood from a sacrifice upon the Ark of the Covenant and move God's hand to forgive Israel of the sins they committed during the entire previous year. This picture gives us an indication of a human being able to pass through the Cherubimic barrier into the Garden again, when compared with the thought of the Garden's entrance barred by Cherubims!

The stipulation involved in the High Priest's ceremony for Israel was that such an entrance beyond the veil could only occur once every year, and nobody else could go with him. One man could enter only during one day a year. True, it was not the actual Garden of Eden into which he entered, but it was undoubtedly a symbolic representation of the Garden! It was associated with a thought of the remedy for the entire problem of man's sin that came upon all of us due to Adam's transgression in the Garden. However, since it was not actually the Garden in which Adam once dwelt, we know that mankind did not have a representative enter the true Garden when the High Priest entered that Holiest of Holies. Nevertheless, God still provided us with this undeniable association to the Garden's story of man's fall.

What was God thinking?

The picture of this man's passage into the Holiest foreshadows the real thing yet to come, as were all the Old Testament rituals of religion. God would not leave man outside and away from His most holy presence! Something was coming that would bring salvation to the human race and recover us into fellowship with God in the Garden once again.

This approach through the veil was a foreshadow of God's plan that would allow mankind back into the Garden where he could approach the Tree of Life, pluck its fruit, eat and live forever! In short, Christ's salvation for mankind was represented in all these rituals, and was based upon the picture of the Garden and the Tree of Life. After all, that scenario in the Garden was the entire reason for the need of man's salvation.

NOT WITHOUT BLOOD

Another very important aspect of this portrait in symbol was the fact that the High Priest could not pass the veil *without blood*.

The New Testament Book of Hebrews shows how the rituals of Old Testament religion were actually wonderful portraits in symbol of the New Testament's spiritual experiences to be had through faith (Hebrews 9:23). The God of the Old Testament is the same God of the New Testament. His ultimate plan has not changed. And in speaking of the particular issue of the passing through the veil into the Holiest, experienced by the High Priest, we are told the High Priest did not enter the Holiest place without blood (Hebrews 9:7).

We also read that God's Spirit inspired this ritual for Israel in order to relay a special message *to us*, today!

> *The Holy Ghost this signifying, that the way into the holiest of all was not yet made manifest, while as the first Tabernacle was yet standing: Hebrews 9:8*

Here, we are told the picture of the High Priest's sole admission into this holy place represents a situation in which, for all practical intents and purposes, God had not yet removed the barrier to the most holy place for mankind in general. If the Holiest Place represents the Garden (and it does), and this ancient ritual allowed only one man into the holiest (and that only once a year), we see that actual entrance into *the Garden* was not yet made manifest. In other words, man was still not allowed the benefits of being able to enter the Garden any more than Adam was allowed to go in to the Tree of Life and get its fruit. This portrayal in the days of the Tabernacle was merely symbolic of the great deliverance that was yet to come.

The verse reads, "The Holy Ghost this signifying." This is the basis for our opportunity to be able to discover symbolism in the Tabernacle picture. The Tabernacle ritual *signified,* or symbolized, something most spiritual. The Spirit of God instructed Moses to have a High Priest carry out the particular ritual. Having done so, the Holy Ghost signified something spiritual, of which the ritual was only a figure (Hebrews 9:9), or a pattern (Hebrews 9:23).

Additional insight is gained when we consider how the forehead of that High Priest was to be covered with a golden plate emblazoned with the words HOLINESS UNTO THE LORD upon it (Exodus 28:36). One had to be holy in order to enter the Garden! No wonder Adam was cast out after he sinned! He was holy beforehand, but, after having sinned he was rendered quite unholy.

WHY WAS A VEIL CHOSEN?

Then there is the question as to why the barrier of Cherubims in the Garden was represented with a *veil*. Why a veil? We know the veil had images of Cherubims sewn into it. But why a veil? One might consider the thought that a veil embroidered with pictures of Cherubims, suspended over an entrance, was the only manner in which one could have symbolized Cherubims that blocked an entrance as in the Garden. Yet it seems there is something more to it than that, due to the following verse, speaking of Christ's sacrificial death:

> *By a new and living way, which he hath consecrated for us, through the veil, that is to say, his flesh;*
> *Hebrews 10:20*

Hebrews Chapter 9 just told us how the High Priest's entrance into the Holiest foreshadowed, or prefigured, entering the Heavenly Garden. We read about the veil representing Christ's flesh only one chapter later.

15

Why would Christ's flesh be involved in this picture? According to this verse (and this is tremendously enlightening) we know God had Christ's *flesh* in mind way back in time when God told Moses to make a veil for the Tabernacle. But why Christ's *flesh*? How would His flesh be associated the barrier in the Garden?

To understand this we must consider the general subject of sin. Paul told us that something called "sin" was in a particular location of his very personal being, after having analyzed a plight he experienced in his attempts to please God legalistically. In Romans Chapter 5, he said Adam turned us all into sinners before we were even born. And now in Chapter 7, we read:

> *Now then it is no more I that do it, but sin that dwelleth in me. For I know that in me (that is, in my flesh,) dwelleth no good thing: for to will is present with me; but how to perform that which is good I find not.*
> *Romans 7:17-18*

In his maddening dilemma of having tried all he knew to do what he considered was good, but finding him sinning instead, Paul recognized the source of his trouble was not himself, directly. It was something *alien* inside him, apart from his personal self, that he called "sin". Sin was in his flesh. Due to this presence of sin, Jesus Christ came.

> *For what the law could not do, in that it was weak through the flesh, God sending his own Son in the likeness of sinful flesh, and for sin, condemned sin in the flesh: That the righteousness of the law might be fulfilled in us,*

16

who walk not after the flesh, but after the Spirit.
Romans 8:3-4

God sent His Son in the likeness of sinful flesh. He came for the reason of sin. He did this to condemn sin in that flesh. Jesus Christ took sin within His own flesh, that he might nullify it in our flesh.

Notice how the words concerning atonement from Leviticus 1:4 come into play here when we read...

For he hath made him to be sin for us, who knew no sin;
that we might be made the righteousness of God in him.
2 Corinthians 5:21

The sacrifice was offered for the person presenting it as Christ was made sin for us. Christ knew no sin. However, He *became sin* for us. In other words, He hanged in our places on the cross. When they crucified His body, they killed the flesh in which He received the sin that exists in our flesh. This, in itself, was a real miracle! Having done so, God condemned sin in the flesh. Sin formerly condemned us (Romans 8:1), but God condemned the *condemner*. He condemned sin!

That is the reason the Temple veil was torn in two at the very moment Jesus Christ died.

And Jesus cried with a loud voice, and gave up the ghost.
And the veil of the Temple was rent in twain from the top
to the bottom. Mark 15:37-38

17

TAKE A BITE OF ETERNAL LIFE

The veil, with Cherubims embroidered into it, was removed! Praise God, the barrier was removed! Since the likeness of Cherubims was sewn into the veil that was rent, and that barrier represented the one that kept Adam from the Tree of Life, we see a wonderful picture of the removal of the Garden's barrier. It was as though the Cherubims departed from the Garden entrance and no longer kept the way of the tree of life when Jesus died and the veil was ripped in two pieces!

Formerly, man's sin made it impossible for him to actually survive, should he pass into the holiest. His entrance into the Garden while still retaining sin would mean his death. Remember that the High Priest had to wear "Holiness Unto the Lord" upon his brow when he entered that room. Man's sin kept man from approaching God. Without holiness no man shall see the Lord.

Is it any wonder the High Priest could not pass the veil without blood? The High Priest's requirement of blood prefigured Christ's atoning death that made it possible for humanity to pass the Cherubims! And the same book of Hebrews, that informed us how the High Priest could not pass the veil without blood, said this about Jesus:

> *Seeing then that we have a great high priest, that is passed into the heavens, Jesus the Son of God, let us hold fast our profession. Hebrews 4:14*

Jesus is our Great High Priest! As the High Priest passed the veil into the Most Holy Place, Christ passed into the heavens after His resurrection and ascension.

PASSING BY THE CHERUBIMS

It all comes together so beautifully! Since sin entered Adam's flesh when he sinned, as realized due to Paul's description of sin existing in our flesh, it can be said that our own *flesh* thereby formed a barrier to the tree of Life. We all know how the Bible taught us about the impulse in our flesh that tends towards sin. Sin was in the flesh, and due to that sin, Adam was rendered unholy and could not dwell in the Most Holy Place of the Garden. In other words, flesh, with sin inside, became *our barrier from Life*. The veil represented that!

Also, the Life within the Tree and its fruit was God's Life, itself. Recall that God simply does not *have* eternal Life, but He *is* eternal Life. Nothing in this creation is eternal. By virtue of the fact that creation was created, it had a beginning and, therefore, cannot be considered "eternal", nor even rendered eternal. People forget that "eternal" is defined as having *no beginning* as well as no ending. If we never die, we are not necessarily eternal. We still had a beginning. Only the Source of creation can be eternal. Only God is eternal.

Adam would have actually placed God's Life within himself had he eaten of the Tree of Life! And here we have another very good reason why God did not want him to eat of the Tree of Life after man sinned. Adam was rendered unclean and unholy, and God did not allow His Holy Spirit to indwell something sinful and unholy!

Since Adam's own flesh became a barrier for him, not allowing him inside the Garden due to its sinfulness, God sent His Son in the likeness of that sinful flesh, when He remained yet without sin. It was, therefore, flesh that could receive sin, though. The Son took our sin within His flesh when He

19

drank the cup in another Garden called Gethsemane, and was later crucified. The death of the cross killed the body that possessed my sin that He took upon Himself. Hence, He became sin *for us*.

> *For he hath made him to be sin for us, who knew no sin; that we might be made the righteousness of God in him.*
> *2 Corinthians 5:21*

This death actually condemned our sin in the flesh of the Son of God. Jesus' body dealt with sin *in the flesh*. Since my inclusion into the Body of Christ, I can claim the privileges of all that Christ's body enjoyed through death. His body became freed from any domination of sin, in His death, and that is why we can say we were freed from sin *through Christ*, or through His death. His death counted as our own, making His subsequent Life's benefits our own as well!

The Apostle Paul once battled with the efforts to live a life without sinning, and related that battle to us in the seventh chapter of Romans. There, he recounted the manner in which he came to realize he was already freed from sin through Christ's death. Sin remains in our flesh even after we are saved, although we are already delivered from the domination of sin over our lives (Romans 6:2, 7, 12, 14). It's in our mortal bodies, but we do not have to let it reign in our mortal bodies. And yet, it will reign if we do not know how to deal with it. Paul wrote about coming into the understanding that there is way to live above sin without struggling to cease sinning, even though sin remains in our flesh! He came to the conclusion that sin is still in our flesh, and we simply must be delivered from this body of death if we ever hope to be freed from that sin. We just have to die! How on earth can that occur, though? If we died, we might pay the penalty for sin, but what good is that if we cannot live to enjoy such freedom? Paul discovered such freedom is actually available in a way one would never have guessed. We are freed from our bodies of death *through the death of the body of Christ on the cross!*

Read it again: Thanks to God, we are freed from our bodies of death through the death of the body of Christ on the cross!

> *O wretched man that I am! who shall deliver me from the body of this death? I thank God through Jesus Christ our Lord. So then with the mind I myself serve the law of God; but with the flesh the law of sin. Romans 7:24-25*

How can it be? We are dead to sin through Christ's body but yet we struggle with sin. Should we not cease from the struggle if we are indeed dead to sin already? The truth is that we have to qualify for the Law of the Spirit of Life to operate and empower us above the strength of sin, before we will enjoy victory, although we did die to it.

Paul explained that Christ's death was accomplished *as our deaths.* We can actually say we died through the death of the body of Christ. That is what it means to say we have been baptized *into His death* (Romans 6:3). Baptism into His death makes that death count as *our deaths,* so far as sin is concerned. That is how God sees it. That is how it actually is. That means we already made the payment for sin, and yet are still able to live to enjoy its benefits. We can, therefore, actually claim the privileges that Christ enjoyed as being freed from any other dominating power when He died on the cross, since we were placed into *union with Christ* and became *the Body of Christ*. Sin is cheated and nullified in our flesh when we understand this mighty revelation of victory, and thereby begin to *walk after the Spirit*.

"Walking after the Spirit" simply refers to the experience of living our lives based upon the truths that God's Word teaches us concerning our freedom from sin through Christ's death. When we face temptation, where sin would normally rise up and see us fall, we can stand upon our union with Christ's death instead, and resist it. We can claim that we were freed from the bondage of sin, and *enforce* that fact. We can call upon God's Spirit of resurrection to work in our lives and strengthen us to overcome sin! Should we fail to stand in faith in this manner, especially due to lack of awareness of it, we will inevitably resort to resistance in our own human strength, and subsequently fail. That failure is due to what is called "walking after the flesh" – or, not complying with the "Law of the Spirit of Life" in living by the truths the bible says we can live by. When we live as though we did not unite to Christ's death and were made free from sin's domination, then that is what Paul called "walking after the flesh." It is the bane of many, many believers today. It is dealing with sin through our own weak, human power, which is all that anyone can know who has not been taught about the Law of the Spirit of Life.

This is the reason the veil, which typified the flesh, was ripped when Christ died! The very reason for the fleshly barrier's existence was put out of the way! We can say that we were crucified and have experienced the rending of our personal barriers of flesh *with Christ's death*.

22

PASSING BY THE CHERUBIMS

Every year the High Priest passed the veil. Naturally, it could not be ripped every year. If it ripped annually, it would have to be replaced, erected and bypassed again the following year. You see, the blood that the High Priest took with him past the veil removed the effects of Israel's sin for only one year. That is the reason it had to be repeated every year. So we can see that their ritual did not fully deal with sin as sin had to eventually be dealt with if man was ever going to be saved from sin.

The reading of Hebrews 10 reveals the very thought of sin having not actually been dealt with as we required, back in the Old Testament days.

> *For the law having a shadow of good things to come, and not the very image of the things, can never with those sacrifices which they offered year by year continually make the comers thereunto perfect. For then would they not have ceased to be offered? because that the worshippers once purged should have had no more conscience of sins. But in those sacrifices there is a remembrance again made of sins every year. For it is not possible that the blood of bulls and of goats should take away sins. Hebrews 10:1-4*

The sacrifices for sin back in those days simply could not cut it. Evidence of this was the fact that the sacrifices had to be repeated over and over again. However, when Christ died as a sacrifice, He forever solved the sin problem, and therefore died only once.

> *By the which will we are sanctified through the offering of the body of Jesus Christ once for all. And every priest standeth daily ministering and offering oftentimes the same*

23

sacrifices, which can never take away sins: But this man, after he had offered one sacrifice for sins for ever, sat down on the right hand of God; From henceforth expecting till his enemies be made his footstool. For by one offering he hath perfected for ever them that are sanctified. Hebrews 10:10-14

Jesus' offering of blood did what the Old Law's offerings could never do. It *remitted* sin.

Now where remission of these is, there is no more offering for sin. Hebrews 10:18

Jesus' death, then, is the fulfillment for the need for us to representatively have someone pass the Cherubims, approach the tree of life, pluck a fruit of Life and give it to us to eat!

SPOTLESS OFFERING

The sacrificial offering had to be without spot or blemish in order to successfully deal with sin, albeit in the meager manner in which it could be dealt with in Old Testament times.

And the LORD said unto Moses, Speak unto Aaron thy brother, that he come not at all times into the holy place within the veil before the mercy seat, which is upon the ark; that he die not: for I will appear in the cloud upon the mercy seat. Thus shall Aaron come into the holy place: with a young bullock for a sin offering, and a ram for a burnt offering. Leviticus 16:2-3

PASSING BY THE CHERUBIMS

And he shall take of the blood of the bullock, and sprinkle it with his finger upon the mercy seat eastward; and before the mercy seat shall he sprinkle of the blood with his finger seven times. Then shall he kill the goat of the sin offering, that is for the people, and bring his blood within the veil, and do with that blood as he did with the blood of the bullock, and sprinkle it upon the mercy seat, and before the mercy seat: Leviticus 16:14-15

A bullock, ram and some goats were the atonement sacrifices. Pay particular notice to the involvement of a ram, or thought of a lamb, in this atonement.

Jesus was not just a High Priest who offered a sacrifice, though! He was all that and much more!

How much more shall the blood of Christ, who through the eternal Spirit offered himself without spot to God, purge your conscience from dead works to serve the living God? Hebrews 9:14

He "offered Himself"! He was the sacrifice as well as the High Priest! How could the sacrifice also be the person of the High Priest at the same time? The answer is that He offered Himself. As the High Priest made the sacrifice of death, he carried its blood into the Most Holy Place. Likewise, Jesus offered Himself, and then He offered His own Blood! He was the High Priest, and He was also the Lamb from whom the High Priest retrieved blood for atonement.

Neither by the blood of goats and calves, but by his own blood he entered in once into the holy place, having obtained eternal redemption for us. Hebrews 9:12

25

TAKE A BITE OF ETERNAL LIFE

In the verse above, we read that *He obtained eternal redemption.* That sounds similar to grabbing hold of the fruit of eternal Life!

The sin that barricaded us from Life was cleansed away from our flesh by the blood of Jesus. This occurred to such an extent that it is said that our very *consciences* are sprinkled from an evil state! We do not even have to *feel* worried or give further thought about our sins any more. In the Old Testament days, the atonement did not remove sins, but each year the people had their sins thrown back into their faces and were required to come good for them by sheer virtue of requiring another sacrifice. However, Jesus Christ took our sins once and for all. We never need worry about our past sins being thrown into our faces again! We never have to deal with them anymore.

Since sin kept us from the Garden, it now can be said that He cleansed us of sin so that we could enter the Garden again as soon as we are initially saved! Access to the Tree of Life has been reinstated!

Jesus, in effect, walked past the Cherubims, plucked a fruit from the Tree of Life, cleansed us and summoned us to come in behind Him so He could give the fruit to us to eat! Rather than leaving man sinful, since the time when Eve first plucked the forbidden fruit and gave to her husband, Jesus removed our sin. He then plucked the fruit of Life and already gave it to us who believe! We can now enjoy eternal life due to Christ's death! We can rule and reign with Him in this life.

3

WHEN JESUS PASSED THE VEIL

After Jesus rose from the dead, Mary was the first one to meet Him in the Garden. He said something most strange to her, but which was actually something quite enlightening in view of all that we have noted so far.

> *Jesus saith unto her, Touch me not; for I am not yet ascended to my Father: but go to my brethren, and say unto them, I ascend unto my Father, and your Father; and to my God, and your God. John 20:17*

One would think the work of redemption was at least fully accomplished after He rose from the dead, if not the moment He died on the cross, but, not so. After He rose from the dead, the most important work had yet to be done! The cross and His death were just the means for this next act to take place

The blood had to be presented!

Strange as it may sound at first, this statement to Mary makes a whole lot of sense when you understand that Jesus is the High Priest. The High Priest could not be touched when he was to enter the holiest through the veil.

TAKE A BITE OF ETERNAL LIFE

And there shall be no man in the Tabernacle of the congregation when he goeth in to make an atonement in the holy place, until he come out, and have made an atonement for himself, and for his household, and for all the congregation of Israel. Leviticus 16:17

So much ritual and preparation of separation and holiness was accomplished by this man, that the touch of one who was unclean, due to lack of holiness, would have ruined and marred the opportunity for him to enter. The entire preparation would have been rendered to an entire waste of time, for God would not have accepted any sacrifice for atonement from this man had he been tainted by an unclean touch, after having been cleansed, himself, by the elaborate ritual of washings beforehand.

Mary was still sinful when Jesus spoke to her. Yes, Jesus had died, was buried and rose again, but He had not yet ascended to the Father to present the shed blood of the sacrifice in the role as High priest of atonement! And should sinful Mary touch Christ, His holiness would have been marred. Therefore, He told her not to touch Him, for He had not yet ascended to the Father – He had not yet entered the holiest to accomplish the great goal!

In effect, Jesus was on His way to pass the Cherubims and approach the Tree of Life! Once there, He would pluck its fruit and give it to humanity. This very action is patterned, not in the first book in the Bible called Genesis, but in the final book called Revelation. How pertinent!

PAST THE CHERUBIMIC BARRIER

If you look carefully, you will find that every picture in the Book of Revelation is actually borrowed from the Old Testament stories and events. And if you read those pictures in Revelation and search the Old Testament from which they were derived, you will recognize a message about Jesus Christ and His church, including the blessings Christ has provided for you.

> *And immediately I was in the spirit; and, behold, a throne was set in heaven, and one sat on the throne.*
> *Revelation 4:2*

John saw a revelation and vision of the Throne of God in Heaven. One sat on that throne.

This reminds us of Adam's place in the Garden from which he was to rule and have dominion over the earth. God gave Adam dominion over all the earth. Of course, John saw God's throne in Heaven in his vision, but is not man made in God's image to rule with God in the earth? As much as God rules in the spiritual realm, was not Adam to rule with God in the physical realm?

Notice the vision of the throne and its surroundings.

> *And before the throne there was a sea of glass like unto crystal: and in the midst of the throne, and round about the throne, were four Beasts full of eyes before and behind. And the first Beast was like a lion, and the second Beast like a calf, and the third Beast had a face as a man, and the fourth Beast was like a flying eagle. Revelation 4:6*

29

TAKE A BITE OF ETERNAL LIFE

Around the throne were four Beasts. Their faces were those of a lion, ox, man and eagle. If you read Ezekiel 10:14, there they were said to be the faces of the Cherubims! (Once again, recall that it was "Cherubims" that blocked the Garden entrance!) John saw Cherubims around the throne! He saw a *Cherubimic* barrier blocking access to the throne of God! They kept the way to the throne as they kept the way of the Tree of Life.

> *Then I looked, and, behold, in the firmament that was above the head of the Cherubims there appeared over them as it were a sapphire stone, as the appearance of the likeness of a throne. Ezekiel 10:1*

Above, we read Ezekiel saw the same throne John saw, with Cherubims around it.

> *And every one had four faces: the first face was the face of a cherub, and the second face was the face of a man, and the third the face of a lion, and the fourth the face of an eagle. Ezekiel 10:14*

These were the creatures he saw in Ezekiel Chapter 1. (The term "cherub" in Ezekiel 10 is replaced by "ox" in chapter 1.)

> *As for the likeness of their faces, they four had the face of a man, and the face of a lion, on the right side: and they four had the face of an ox on the left side; they four also had the face of an eagle. Ezekiel 1:10*

John saw a Cherubimic barrier just as we find in Genesis.

30

Instead of a Tree of Life, though, Ezekiel saw them protecting man from access to a Throne! And God sat on that Throne. God is not dangerous, but His glory is so intense that sinful humanity would be annihilated by it if man approached Him in his sin.

God told Moses about this very thing.

And he said, Thou canst not see my face: for there shall no man see me, and live. Exodus 33:20

God had to hide Moses in a cleft of the rock in order to allow him to see only the back parts of the glory. Had Moses stepped out and seen the full force of glory, he would have instantly died.

In the hand of God, past the Cherubims, was a little sealed book (Revelation 5:1)! Then John heard a strong angel cry for a worthy one to come and take the book!

This can only mean one thing!

Since mankind required somebody to pass the Cherubims of the Garden entrance and proceed to the tree of life and pluck its fruit, for their restoration to God, we see a cry made in Revelation for one to pass the Beasts, go to the throne of God and take the little book! What a perfect picture of our need for salvation! This is a parallel vision of the need for man to go to the tree of life and pluck its fruit! Here, Revelation is showing us a pattern of salvation based upon the Garden of Eden's tragedy, and using a pattern of those pictures in Genesis to relate to us of how the work of the cross saves us.

TAKE A BITE OF ETERNAL LIFE

As we follow the picture in Revelation, we know it is God's will for man to return and take the book since an angel invited a worthy one to come!

And no man in heaven, nor in earth, neither under the earth, was able to open the book, neither to look thereon. Revelation 5:3

Just as with the Garden in Genesis, no man was worthy to approach and pass the Beasts to take the book in Revelation. Why? No man could pass due to sin, of course! After all, Adam was driven out and could not return back inside, past the Cherubims, due to his sin. His sin kept him from the Tree of Life.

And I wept much, because no man was found worthy to open and to read the book, neither to look thereon. Revelation 5:4

No wonder John wept much! Due to Adam's sin, man figuratively was left outside the Garden, as nobody could enter this throne-room in Heaven, and was unable to return to pluck the fruit of life symbolized by the retrieval of the little sealed book! What a state of sorrow! All of this symbolically shows a sinner lost and without God today.

And one of the elders saith unto me, Weep not: behold, the Lion of the tribe of Juda, the Root of David, hath prevailed to open the book, and to loose the seven seals thereof. Revelation 5:5

Weep not? Does this mean someone is worthy? Can someone pass the Beasts?

32

Yes! The lion of the tribe of Judah prevailed to open the book! John whirled around to look.

> *And I beheld, and, lo, in the midst of the throne and of the four Beasts, and in the midst of the elders, stood a Lamb as it had been slain, having seven horns and seven eyes, which are the seven Spirits of God sent forth into all the earth. Revelation 5:6*

Praise God! Note the phrase, "In the midst of the throne and the four Beasts!" This is more clearly translated as saying "...between the Beasts, who blocked mankind, and the throne, which represented the tree of life, stood a Lamb!"

Someone passed the Beasts! Someone passed the *Cherubimic* barrier and was inside the Garden! It was a Lamb!

Was not one called upon to approach the throne and take the book?

Yes.

Was there a "man" found worthy to come?

Oh, yes!

A LAMB

Then why is a lamb here?

John the Baptist called Jesus the "Lamb of God" Who takes away the sins of the world. He was not only the High Priest who offered a lamb, but He offered Himself. The true

High Priest, Jesus Christ, is also the Lamb! The Lamb is the only man worthy in a world where nobody else was ever found worthy to enter the Garden!

This lamb was slain! Atonement sacrifice was made. Blood was supplied so that someone might pass the veil to indicate that a required death had occurred. This lamb was slain, but was raised from death. Recall the Lamb "had been slain" but yet was seen standing! That is resurrection! This vision represented the great resurrection of Christ which occurred 2,000 years ago! Jesus told John to write about the past, present and future – not just the future! And this is the most wonderful event of all history's past!

> *Write the things which thou hast seen, and the things which are, and the things which shall be hereafter;* Revelation 1:19

It was necessary to show John these things in order to reveal to him the entire plan of God through symbolism, so that we might have this wonderful presentation from which to glean mighty truths! How else can we understand the great plan for all of time without seeing a vision of what happened when Jesus rose from the dead?

Mary actually spoke to the same Lamb who was slain and risen to stand again, when she came to anoint His body and then spoke to the resurrected Jesus! But that Lamb had not yet passed the barrier when she found Him. He was just on His way there, so Mary could not touch Him. The High Priest/Lamb was on His way into the Holiest to pluck from the tree of life and give eternal life to mankind! Revelation chapter 5 offers the pattern of the events that transpired im-

34

mediately following the moments we read about in John 20 when Jesus spoke to Mary.

SEVEN HORNS

When Jesus Christ resurrected and spoke for forty days about the Kingdom of God (Acts 1:2), among those words He said the following:

> *And Jesus came and spake unto them, saying, All power is given unto me in heaven and in earth. Matthew 28:18*

Jesus had all power. When John saw Him represented as a Lamb, he saw that the Lamb had seven horns. The number seven implies completeness or fullness. And a horn is indicative of power in the Bible. Jesus had seven horns, or all power, and He particularly declared this truth after He rose from the dead. He was slain and rose again and claimed to have all power in heaven and in earth, just as John saw Him as a Lamb resurrected with seven horns.

SEVEN EYES

John also noted that the Lamb had seven eyes. This, too, is indicative of His role as High Priest.

> *For the word of God is quick, and powerful, and sharper than any twoedged sword, piercing even to the dividing asunder of soul and spirit, and of the joints and marrow, and is a discerner of the thoughts and intents of the heart. Neither is there any creature that is not manifest in his sight: but all things are naked and opened unto the eyes of him with whom we have to do. Seeing then that we*

have a great high priest, that is passed into the heavens,
Jesus the Son of God, let us hold fast our profession.
Hebrews 4:12-14

Our High Priest sees all things. Nothing is hidden from Him. All things are "naked and opened unto the eyes of him with whom we have to do." This is the meaning behind the symbol of the seven eyes. And He is distinctly known as High Priest when this characteristic is mentioned in Hebrews 4, thus clearly linking together the vision of John with the truth of the High Priesthood of Jesus Christ.

Seven eyes also intimate all wisdom. Wisdom is the characteristic that allows one to understand properly. When one has wisdom, one is aware of that of which many people are not made aware. Solomon was aware of what to do when two harlots presented him with a single baby, while both women claimed to be the mother. Knowing that a true mother would sacrifice anything to allow her child to live, Solomon watched the women's reactions when he ordered the baby to be cut in two and each piece be given to each "mother." The woman who sacrificed her pleasure in keeping the baby offered to allow the other to have the child, thus informing Solomon she was the actual mother.

Jesus has all (7) wisdom (eyes). Nothing is unknown to Him. He sees all. There is no mystery He does not know. In the Bible, "mystery" was the term used to describe a truth not yet revealed to mankind. The entire plan of salvation was referred to as a mystery by the Apostle Paul in Ephesians Chapter 1 and Chapter 3 before Jesus came and the Church was born so we could understand this mystery. Colossians chapter 1 refers to "the riches of the mystery" which were hidden "from ages and from generations but now is made manifest to the saints." Even Jesus said, "Unto you it is given to know the mystery of the Kingdom of God, but unto them that are without; all these things are done in parables" (Mark 4:11). Paul said that blindness happened to Israel for a period of time, after which the nation shall again know Him, for the purpose that Gentiles might be born again. He referred to that plan as a "mystery" revealed through his ministry (Romans 11:25).

The Gospel and preaching of Jesus Christ was a mystery kept secret since the beginning of the world (Romans 16:25). One who was not kept from a mystery was said to be one who possessed "wisdom" concerning it.

> *To whom God would make known what is the riches of the glory of this mystery among the Gentiles; which is Christ in you, the hope of glory: Whom we preach, warning every man, and teaching every man in all wisdom; that we may present every man perfect in Christ Jesus:*
> *Colossians 1:27-28*

The book of Ephesians reads of God abounding towards us in all wisdom, having made known unto us the mystery of His will (Ephesians 1:8-9).

So, seven eyes represent all wisdom. He has all wisdom and all power.

The book of Ephesians chapter 1 reads about the wisdom God had in giving us understanding, and then relates the almighty power of Jesus Christ. He is raised above every

name. He is above all power and principality. All things are
put under His feet. All -- all -- all. Seven -- seven -- seven.

LOOKING FOR A LION,
BUT FINDING A LAMB

But notice John was told to behold the Lion of Judah
who prevailed to open the book. Why did John see a Lamb,
with seven eyes and horns at that, when he was told to behold a lion? What could be more diverse from a lion than a
lamb? There would be no greater an example of meekness
and weakness than in the picture of a lamb.

The message is that the greatest and boldest act of courage was accomplished by the greatest manner of meekness
one could imagine. By submitting to the obedience of death,
the greatest form of sacrifice and weakness, Jesus accomplished the boldest and grandest of all works! The salvation
of all of mankind who would only believe! He died, arose
and appeared in this most Holy Place. The entire focus was
on His retrieval of that Sealed Book

4

JESUS TOOK THE BOOK

*And he came and took the book out of the right hand of
him that sat upon the throne. Revelation 5:7*

Just like taking the fruit of Life from the branch of the
Tree of Life, Jesus took the book from the hand of God
on the throne. Picture the tree of Life as God on the
throne. A fruit in the branch of the Tree would perfectly parallel a book in the hand of God on the throne. And the
Lamb plucked it.

Then suddenly, the very Beasts that blocked unholy humanity from the throne began praising. We must not miss a
note in this picture. The former *blockers* were now rejoicing.

*And when he had taken the book, the four Beasts and
four and twenty elders fell down before the Lamb, having
every one of them harps, and golden vials full of odours,
which are the prayers of saints. And they sung a new
song, saying, Thou art worthy to take the book, and to
open the seals thereof: for thou wast slain, and hast
redeemed us to God by thy blood out of every kindred, and
tongue, and people, and nation; And hast made us unto
our God kings and priests: and we shall reign on the
earth. Revelation 5:8-10*

TAKE A BITE OF ETERNAL LIFE

Praise God! Jesus redeemed mankind by His blood! And whereas Adam was meant to rule the world and have dominion on the earth, he instead lost that dominion and was cast out of his "throne room" called the Garden, due to sin. Jesus passed the barrier, approached the Throne and took the book, thus redeeming us by His blood that we might be kings and reign on the earth once again! Man is representatively seen here returning to his throne-room of the Garden!

Jesus was worthy to open the book. When a book is sealed, it is hidden from the sight of people. This book represents a message and a truth. But it represents a *hidden* truth, since it is sealed. Having seven seals implies a mystery that is completely hidden – but Jesus has seven eyes. In other words, nothing is hid from Him, and no mystery can be unknown by Him. He has all understanding to be able to comprehend all mysteries!

And, oh, did John hear shouts of praise then!

And every creature which is in heaven, and on the earth, and under the earth, and such as are in the sea, and all that are in them, heard I saying, Blessing, and honour, and glory, and power, be unto him that sitteth upon the throne, and unto the Lamb for ever and ever. Revelation 5:13

John heard every living creature shout praises! After all, creation had been held in bondage of corruption ever since its leader, Adam, threw it into sin.

For the creature was made subject to vanity, not willingly, but by reason of him who hath subjected the same in hope,

40

Because the creature itself also shall be delivered from the bondage of corruption into the glorious liberty of the children of God. Romans 8:20-21

John saw someone return to the very place to which mankind needed to return. God, Himself, stood as the Tree of Life in Revelation 5. The Fruit of Life in the tree's branch was represented by the little sealed book in God's hand. And God gave this Life to His Son so that, in turn, it could be given to us! Eternal life! That book has something to do with eternal Life, for it was perfectly paralleled in this vision by the fruit of Life in Genesis!

COME AND SEE

No man was worthy to take the book and to open it and look inside it, but Jesus arrived and did that very thing, only after He rose from the dead, though. God was manifested as a man, Himself (1 Timothy 3:16). He was worthy, for He had no sin. Yet, what good was it for God to hold and read the book, Himself? This would do nothing for mankind. However, we must realize that when Jesus died in flesh, He identified with us and took our sins upon Himself to die as us. And that act freed us from sin so that we could then look at the book! This is exactly what John experienced in the vision. We could enter the Garden, as it were, due to Christ's vicarious atonement.

And I saw when the Lamb opened one of the seals, and I heard, as it were the noise of thunder, one of the four Beasts saying, Come and see. Revelation 6:1

One of the very Beasts that barred mankind later invited John to come, pass them, approach Jesus and take a look in the Book! Only after it was said that Jesus redeemed mankind, could John come and see. Jesus was already holy, but His redemption through His blood for mankind made man holy! Now the Beast could allow John by to see, too!

And I saw... Revelation 6:2

Praise God, John saw! He entered the Garden, in effect, and looked upon the book. He received insight and wisdom and revelation concerning a former mystery. What he saw and the meanings of the visions are not our point for now. The pattern of how he came to see it is what we are concentrating upon.

COME AND EAT

John saw more about this grand vision as is recorded later in Revelation Chapter 10,

> *And I saw another mighty angel come down from heaven,*
> *clothed with a cloud: and a rainbow was upon his head,*
> *and his face was as it were the sun, and his feet as pillars*
> *of fire: Revelation 10:1*

He saw a Mighty Angel descend from Heaven. Notice that this angel was no ordinary angel. It had a face like the sun, and feet like pillars of fire, and a rainbow was around is head. Why, this is none other than Jesus Christ! Notice in Revelation Chapter One that Jesus was described with the very characteristics with which this Mighty Angel was described.

And in the midst of the seven candlesticks one like unto the Son of man, ...And his feet like unto fine brass, as if they burned in a furnace.... Revelation 1:13-15

Jesus has feet like brass, which glowed like fire in Chapter 10.

And was transfigured before them: and his face did shine as the sun, and his raiment was white as the light. Matthew 17:2

In the transfiguration, He had the face of the sun!

And John saw him descend from Heaven with clouds!

Clouds and darkness are round about him: righteousness and judgment are the habitation of his throne. Psalm 97:2

Who layeth the beams of his chambers in the waters: who maketh the clouds his chariot: who walketh upon the wings of the wind: Psalm 104:3

Behold, he shall come up as clouds, and his chariots shall be as a whirlwind: his horses are swifter than eagles. Woe unto us! for we are spoiled. Jeremiah 4:13

I saw in the night visions, and, behold, one like the Son of man came with the clouds of heaven, and came to the Ancient of days, and they brought him near before him. Daniel 7:13

In fact, He is said to return in clouds (1 Thessalonians 4:17; Matthew 24:30).

43

TAKE A BITE OF ETERNAL LIFE

In Revelation 4, John saw a rainbow around the throne of God. This mighty angel had a rainbow around His head! And he roars like a lion as Christ was called the lion of the tribe of Judah in Revelation 5:5.

Did not Jesus tell Mary he was to ascend to His Father while He was to present His blood as High Priest? Here, the Mighty Angel is said to have *descended*! He had been to Heaven and has descended! He had been to the place where the rainbow was situated around the throne. He has *an open book* in His hand! This is none other than the book that was formerly sealed.

The hope of Noah's rainbow, promising no more destruction by a flood, was evidently situated up in Heaven, and come down to earth with Jesus after He entered there and made our Atonement. The rainbow about His head indicates to us that His very *mind* was upon the covenant, as a faithful High Priest.

Although He died as a Lamb before He took the Book, He accomplished the powerful victory we would ascribe to a Lion. He conquered sin and destroyed him who had the power of death, that is, the devil (Hebrews 2:14). This is what the angel in Revelation 10 resembled as He spoke.

And he had in his hand a little book open: and he set his right foot upon the sea, and his left foot on the earth, And cried with a loud voice, as when a lion roareth: and when he had cried, seven thunders uttered their voices. Revelation 10:2-3

The Lion finally has roared after the lamb was led dumb to the slaughter! Ultimate power was accomplished through weakness. The little book was in His hand. It was opened. Figuratively, He also had the fruit of Life in His hand, plucked from the Tree of Life – taken from God the Father.

When the Mighty Angel cried, seven thunders pealed across the sky. Not only was the rainbow in the throne-room in Revelation 4, but thunders sounded forth from that same place as well. Whoever this Mighty Angel was, and it appears to be Jesus, He was in the secret place of thunder! He was in the throne-room, the holy of holies, of Heaven itself!

And out of the throne proceeded lightnings and thunderings and voices: and there were seven lamps of fire burning before the throne, which are the seven Spirits of God. Revelation 4:5

Note that the thunder and a rainbow, associated in chapter 10 with the Mighty Angel, were associated with the throne in Revelation 4. This mighty angel is the High Priest who was previously in the Holy of Holies in Revelation 5.

The thought of the Mighty Angel being Jesus Christ, Himself, is further witnessed by looking at the angel's words throughout the 10th and 11th Chapters of Revelation.

And I took the little book out of the angel's hand, and ate it up; and it was in my mouth sweet as honey: and as soon as I had eaten it, my belly was bitter. And he said unto me, Thou must prophesy again before many peoples, and nations, and tongues, and kings. And there was given me a reed like unto a rod: and the angel stood, saying, Rise, and measure the Temple of God, and the altar, and them that worship therein. But the court which is without the Temple leave out, and measure it not; for it is given unto the Gentiles: and the holy city shall they tread under foot forty and two months And I will give power unto my two witnesses, and they shall prophesy a thousand two hundred and threescore days, clothed in sackcloth. Revelation 10:10-11:3

The same angel who gave John the book to eat also spoke to John, and among other things said, "I will give power unto my two witnesses," as he referred to the two olive trees in 11:3-4. He said "my" witnesses. Do normal angels have witnesses? Clearly these two prophets mentioned as witnesses give their testimony concerning Jesus Christ, and not about any regular angel!

Several scholars affirm this angel to be a symbol of Jesus Christ, also. For the sake of confirmation, let us quote these words from <u>Matthew Henry's Concise Commentary on the Whole Bible</u> regarding the Mighty Angel:

> "The apostle saw another representation. The person communicating this discovery probably was our Lord and Saviour Jesus Christ, or it was to show his glory. He veils his glory, which is too great for mortal eyes to behold; and throws a veil upon his dispensations. A rainbow was upon his head; our Lord is always mindful of his covenant. His awful voice was echoed by seven thunders; solemn and terrible ways of discovering the mind of God."

JESUS TOOK THE BOOK

And from The People's New Testament Commentary of Him:

> "I saw another mighty angel come down from heaven." This mighty angel was seen in vision and is to be regarded as a symbol. The description is very much like that of the Son of Man in Revelation 1:13-16
>
> While the whole may signify some momentous movement the similarity of the description implies that Christ comes in that movement. Let the facts stated be observed closely.
>
> He is a mighty angel.
>
> He comes down from heaven, enveloped in a cloud.
>
> The rainbow about his head is the symbol of hope and peace.
>
> The shining of his face and feet indicate that he shall spread light and intelligence.
>
> His standing on sea and land shows that his mission was to the whole world.
>
> The angel holds in his hand an open book. The roll is not only unsealed, but it is unrolled so that it can be read. This open book occupies a very conspicuous place in his work. The book in the angel's hand must be an emblem of some fact.

> The seventh fact is that when he, standing on
> land and sea, with the open book in his hand,
> cried in a loud voice, a command, or
> proclamation, or a call for attention, the seven
> thunders uttered their voices. The whole
> evidently signifies some mighty movement on
> the earth inaugurated by Christ.

Jesus distinctly took the book out of the right hand of
Him that sat on the throne in Revelation 5 and proceeded to
open that sealed book. This further corroborates the position
that this is indeed Jesus with the same book now completely
opened! The very first verse in this book of Revelation stated
that the man Christ Jesus was given a revelation by God to be
given to His servants. As Son of God, Jesus was a messenger. An Angel is literally a "messenger". Even the pastors of
the seven churches were called an "angel" in each letter at-
tributed to them in Revelation chapters 2 and 3. When these
angels were addressed, we read of several rebukes to them,
and their need to repent. Surely a heavenly angel is not addressed there with need to repent.

Let us return to the scenario in Revelation 10. Next we
read how John experienced something most wonderful!

> *And I went unto the angel, and said unto him, Give me*
> *the little book. And he said unto me, Take it, and eat it*
> *up; and it shall make thy belly bitter, but it shall be in*
> *thy mouth sweet as honey. Revelation 10:9*

It all comes together now! Think about Revelation 5 and
the initial retrieval of the Book from the right hand of God.
In walking past the Cherubimic veil of four Beasts, Jesus en-

tered the Garden of the throne-room and took the eternal
fruit in the form of the sealed book from the branch of God's
right hand to show it to John. He then descended to earth
and allowed John to come and take the book of eternal life
from Him and proceed to eat of it! John took a bite out of
eternal life! And, oh, it was a spiritual fruit indeed! For in
taking a bite of it, something happened!

> *And I took the little book out of the angel's hand, and*
> *ate it up; and it was in my mouth sweet as honey: and as*
> *soon as I had eaten it, my belly was bitter.*
> *Revelation 10:10*

This same thing occurred with Ezekiel in one of his visions:

> *Moreover he said unto me, Son of man, eat that thou*
> *findest; eat this roll, and go speak unto the house of Israel.*
> *So I opened my mouth, and he caused me to eat that roll.*
> *And he said unto me, Son of man, cause thy belly to eat,*
> *and fill thy bowels with this roll that I give thee. Then*
> *did I eat it; and it was in my mouth as honey for*
> *sweetness. Ezekiel 3:1-3*

> *So the spirit lifted me up, and took me away, and I went*
> *in bitterness, in the heat of my spirit; but the hand of the*
> *LORD was strong upon me. Ezekiel 3:14*

Ezekiel described the same feeling of bitterness John felt
in his belly and called it the "heat of my spirit." There are
many parallels between the prophecy of Ezekiel and that of
John's Revelation. (The student might wish to dig deeply into
Ezekiel with the thoughts of Revelation in mind, to discover

many other parallel passages from the front of each book to their end!) The belly represents the spirit of a man (Proverbs 18:14). It is the candle of the Lord – to be lit with fire of God's Spirit. It burns and experiences heat. John experienced his spirit become heated and made bitter. It lit his spirit alive and on fire and enraged John with a holy anger against sin! The candle's cold wick was made alive with flames of God's Spirit when he ate that book. Indeed, not an ordinary fruit is this fruit of Life! While the forbidden fruit affected the woman in the Garden in a most spiritual manner, so was John affected by the eating of the fruit of Life, in the form of the little book! Ezekiel was told to speak to Israel, but first he must eat the roll. So, too, was John told to eat the book and then to prophesy!

> *And I took the little book out of the angel's hand, and ate it up; and it was in my mouth sweet as honey: and as soon as I had eaten it, my belly was bitter. And he said unto me, Thou must prophesy again before many peoples, and nations, and tongues, and kings. Revelation 10:10-11*

The eating of the book so spiritually affected John that it enabled him to prophesy, as it did Ezekiel! And if the book is devoured by a person to affect one to prophesy, certainly eating the book or the fruit of Life actually instills inspiration of truth.

We must all receive truth into our lives and then tell others. John was given truth and he ate it!

Someone once wrote a hymn singing, "Where He leads I'll follow." We should add a verse to that, reading, "What

He feeds, I'll swallow." While this entire picture could very well point to a specific judgment, which I think it does, the pattern of truth being preached in a general manner is seen here. Even soteriological (salvational) truth, and all the ramifications involved with the truth of the Gospel, can be considered in this same pattern. It all represents the revelation which God gave to Jesus so that Jesus could give to us!

Eating the fruit of life represents receiving a revelation of truth. It is indeed revelation for it is pictured as a sealed book, and that which is sealed is a mystery and must be revealed. Revealing a thing is the revelation of a thing.

The content of Ezekiel's roll is told to be the following:

And he spread it before me; and it was written within and without: and there was written therein lamentations, and mourning, and woe. Ezekiel 2:10

The Book of Revelation lists much mourning and woe and lamentation, too. Jeremiah gave a roll, similar to Ezekiel's roll of woes and lamentations, to Jehoiakim regarding woes and wrath of God, that Jehoiakim later burned (Jeremiah 36:29-32).

Considering this roll, or "book" as Revelation terms it, it is no coincidence that amongst the revelations from this sealed book that is unsealed, Revelation 8:13 relates the picture of an angel flying through Heaven loudly proclaiming "Woe, woe, woe."

And I beheld, and heard an angel flying through the midst of heaven, saying with a loud voice, Woe, woe, woe,

51

*to the inhabiters of the earth by reason of the other voices
of the trumpet of the three angels, which are yet to sound!*

This seems to be repeated again in Revelation 14:6 as follows:

*And I saw another angel fly in the midst of heaven,
having the everlasting gospel to preach unto them that
dwell on the earth, and to every nation, and kindred, and
tongue, and people,*

In the second picture, the angel is again seen flying through Heaven, but this time proclaims the everlasting Gospel! This links the two thoughts of woe and the Gospel together. It is beyond coincidence that the angel flies through heaven in one point declaring woe, and at another point declaring the everlasting Gospel, for the two thoughts to not be linked together. We indeed do need to see that it is necessary to indicate the state of sorrow that those who disobey the gospel will experience in order to fully appreciate this note.

Could this angel who flew through Heaven be part of a pattern God uses to also apply to the Gospel being prophesied to all the nations after having been given to the church? John was told to prophesy to all nations, and actual heavenly angels were never told to preach the Gospel. This angel symbolized the preaching of the Gospel.

Even Jesus, Himself, referred to the Gospel and judgment together as follows:

*He that believeth and is baptized shall be saved; but he
that believeth not shall be damned. Mark 16:16*

52

THE FATHER GAVE TO THE SON THAT THE SON MIGHT GIVE TO US

Just before Jesus was to be taken by the soldiers and to die on the cross, He prayed as follows to His Father.

> *These words spake Jesus, and lifted up his eyes to heaven, and said, Father, the hour is come; glorify thy Son, that thy Son also may glorify thee: As thou hast given him power over all flesh, that he should give eternal life to as many as thou hast given him. And this is life eternal, that they might know thee the only true God, and Jesus Christ, whom thou hast sent. John 17:1-3*

With Revelation 1:1 in mind (the giving of revelation to Jesus by God in order for Jesus to give it to man), we read very informative and enlightening words here. John wrote this account in his Gospel – the same man who had the vision found in the book of Revelation.

Just as God gave Him the little book, Jesus said that God gave Him power. Then Jesus explained that, having received this power from God, He "should give eternal life to as many as thou hast given him." This is it! This is what taking the fruit of Life and giving it to mankind really means! This is what taking the book and giving it to John to eat patterns forth! It means that eternal life has been given by Jesus to those whom God had given to Jesus. This is Revelation 1:1 all over again!

If we consider the stories and events and truths given to us in the Old and New Testaments, we will find the meanings behind every vision in the Book of Revelation.

TAKE A BITE OF ETERNAL LIFE

Revelation 1:1 reads that God gave Jesus the revelation in order to subsequently give it to his servants. Those people whom God gave to Jesus in John 17:2 are called Jesus' "servants" in Revelation 1:1. Jesus prayed, saying He was ready to give eternal life to His servants, just as Revelation patterned forth the giving of the fruit from the tree of life to mankind!

What is that eternal life? What do the book and fruit represent?

> *And this is life eternal, that they might know thee the only true God, and Jesus Christ, whom thou hast sent. John 17:3*

These things represent the tools we need in order to know God!

Indeed, knowing God is eternal life, for the very lack of that element is the reason some will not enter the Kingdom of God.

In Matthew 7, having spoken about good trees and their fruit, and evil trees (enlightening in the context of this study!), Jesus then proceeded to speak about knowing Him as the means to entering the Kingdom. Keep the entire reason for man's sin in mind when you read these words as follows:

> *Even so every good tree bringeth forth good fruit; but a corrupt tree bringeth forth evil fruit. A good tree cannot bring forth evil fruit, neither can a corrupt tree bring forth good fruit. Every tree that bringeth not forth good fruit is hewn down, and cast into the fire. Wherefore by their*

54

fruits ye shall know them. Not every one that saith unto me, Lord, Lord, shall enter into the kingdom of heaven; but he that doeth the will of my Father which is in heaven. Many will say to me in that day, Lord, Lord, have we not prophesied in thy name? and in thy name have cast out devils? and in thy name done many wonderful works? And then will I profess unto them, I never knew you: depart from me, ye that work iniquity. Matthew 7:17-23

Now, notice that entering the Kingdom is given as the reason the Beasts praised God when Jesus redeemed them, for they said "we shall reign on the earth!" Reigning on earth indicates a kingdom and dominion on earth. Matthew 7:21 mentions entrance into the "kingdom". This is a reference to entrance back into the Kingdom Adam lost. Instead of Adam ruling, though, Jesus is the last man Adam who is King of Kings. We are the "kings" over whom Jesus is King!

It is the glory of God to conceal a thing: but the honour of kings is to search out a matter. Proverbs 25:2

God has concealed these truths and called them "the mystery", intended to be "revealed" as a revelation! He hid, or veiled away (remember the veil with Cherubims that barred the people from the holiest of holies, reminiscent of Adam who was barred from the Garden by Cherubims), the eternal life from sinful humanity. Only those who were re-deemed and have been made Kings have the honour to search out and look into the matter and receive eternal life! The world wants to live forever, but the answer to eternal life is a hidden from them, for they are sinful. But to those who confess their sins and believe that Jesus opened the way through the veil by His death, this eternal life is made available!

The Glory of God has concealed the truth as symbolized by a seven-sealed (seven means complete in the Bible – hence, a completely sealed...) book.

Daniel saw the precise same account in another vision, but something was missing in his version, since it was not to be made known as to *how* God would redeem mankind in Daniel's day. God only said He would. First He saw the Ancient of Days sit on a throne, as God the Father. Then one like the Son of man approaches Him and obtains something from Him.

I beheld till the thrones were cast down, and the Ancient of days did sit, whose garment was white as snow, and the hair of his head like the pure wool: his throne was like the fiery flame, and his wheels as burning fire. A fiery stream issued and came forth from before him: thousand thousands ministered unto him, and ten thousand times ten thousand stood before him: the judgment was set, and the books were opened. Daniel 7:9-10

I saw in the night visions, and, behold, one like the Son of man came with the clouds of heaven, and came to the Ancient of days, and they brought him near before him. And there was given him dominion, and glory, and a kingdom, that all people, nations, and languages, should serve him: his dominion is an everlasting dominion, which shall not pass away, and his kingdom that which shall not be destroyed. Daniel 7:13-14

JESUS TOOK THE BOOK

The Son of Man approached the Ancient of Days and received something, as in Revelation 5. Daniel said He received dominion and glory and a kingdom. And as we read further in this chapter, we find the following:

> *I beheld, and the same horn made war with the saints, and shall prevailed against them; Until the Ancient of days came, and judgment was given to the saints of the most High; and the time came that the saints possessed the kingdom. Daniel 7:21-22*

> *And he shall speak great words against the most High, and shall wear out the saints of the most High, and think to change times and laws: and they shall be given into his hand until a time and times and the dividing of time. But the judgment shall sit, and they shall take away his dominion, to consume and to destroy it unto the end. And the kingdom and dominion, and the greatness of the kingdom under the whole heaven, shall be given to the people of the saints of the most High, whose kingdom is an everlasting kingdom, and all dominions shall serve and obey him. Daniel 7:25-27*

Daniel saw the Son of Man take dominion from the Ancient of days who sat on the throne. Then we read that the Saints of God possess the Kingdom! How can this be? If Jesus took dominion, why do the saints have it?

It is because Jesus took dominion for us, and we became kings and priests! Notice the parallel in the words of John's revelation:

TAKE A BITE OF ETERNAL LIFE

And they sung a new song, saying, Thou art worthy to take the book, and to open the seals thereof: for thou wast slain, and hast redeemed us to God by thy blood out of every kindred, and tongue, and people, and nation; And hast made us unto our God kings and priests: and we shall reign on the earth. Revelation 5:9-10

As Daniel saw Jesus take dominion for the church, John saw Jesus take the book and render the saints as kings and priests! The most momentous event to ever occur with mankind happened when Jesus took the dominion that Adam lost and gave it to all who stand with Him and believe in Him as Redeemer Messiah and Christ.

What Daniel was not shown regarded the manner in which Jesus would redeem us. It was by the blood of the Lamb, or the death of the cross! The all-important element not mentioned in Daniel 7 is the reference to the blood. This was due to the fact that the Gospel plan of salvation was yet a mystery in Daniel's day. It was still sealed (Daniel 12:4, 9)!

5

ETERNAL LIFE BY
WAY OF JESUS

These passages below prove beyond the shadow of a doubt that the Book of Revelation, and the basis of that book in its vision of Christ taking the Book to give it to John, includes a pattern associated with the reception of God's eternal life. Jesus is a messenger (angel) in this sense, as Son of God. One who is given something to relay to another is a messenger, or angel.

All the following scriptures reveal precisely the same manner in which the Father gave the Son the blessed Revelation to give to us, His people, as Revelation 1:1 explained.

(For the life was manifested, and we have seen it, and bear witness, and show unto you that eternal life, which was with the Father, and was manifested unto us;)
1 John 1:2

And we know that the Son of God is come, and hath given us an understanding, that we may know him that is true, and we are in him that is true, even in his Son Jesus Christ. This is the true God, and eternal life.
1 John 5:20

And I give unto them eternal life; and they shall never perish, neither shall any man pluck them out of my hand. John 10:28

For the wages of sin is death; but the gift of God is eternal life through Jesus Christ our Lord. Romans 6:23

But whosoever drinketh of the water that I shall give him shall never thirst; but the water that I shall give him shall be in him a well of water springing up into everlasting life. John 4:14

The secret of the LORD is with them that fear him; and he will show them his covenant. Psalm 25:14

For the Father loveth the Son, and showeth him all things that himself doeth: and he will show him greater works than these, that ye may marvel. John 5:20

Jesus answered them, and said, My doctrine is not mine, but his that sent me. John 7:16

JESUS' LAST WORDS

When Jesus was ready to leave the disciples in His physical body's ascent to Heaven, He met them and gave them these final words concerning their duty:

Then opened he their understanding, that they might understand the scriptures, And said unto them, Thus it is written, and thus it behoved Christ to suffer, and to rise from the dead the third day: And that repentance and remission of sins should be preached in his name among all nations, beginning at Jerusalem. And ye are witnesses of these things. And, behold, I send the promise of my Father upon you: but tarry ye in the city of Jerusalem, until ye be endued with power from on high. Luke 24:45-49

His last words were for them to preach a message.

What words were spoken to John after he ate the little book?

And I took the little book out of the angel's hand, and ate it up; and it was in my mouth sweet as honey: and as soon as I had eaten it, my belly was bitter. And he said unto me, Thou must prophesy again before many peoples, and nations, and tongues, and kings. Revelation 10:10-11

John had to preach to all nations. Jesus told the disciples to preach to all nations after He rose from the dead. As the Lamb was slain and stood in resurrection, Jesus Christ died and rose again. And as the Lion gave John a book to eat and told John to prophesy before many nations, Jesus resurrected and revealed to the disciples a message they were to preach to all nations.

Catch the pattern! This was repeated in the words of Luke 24 after Jesus descended to the earth after having met Mary and ascended to the Father. The disciples had to preach to all nations the message of repentance and remission of sins in Jesus' name. That ministry would begin at Jerusalem. As the Gospel of Luke ends with the account of the discussion, the Book of Acts opens with it.

61

The former treatise have I made, O Theophilus, of all that Jesus began both to do and teach, Until the day in which he was taken up, after that he through the Holy Ghost had given commandments unto the apostles whom he had chosen: To whom also he showed himself alive after his passion by many infallible proofs, being seen of them forty days, and speaking of the things pertaining to the kingdom of God: And, being assembled together with them, commanded them that they should not depart from Jerusalem, but wait for the promise of the Father, which, saith he, ye have heard of me. Acts 1:1-4

He mentioned the promise of the Father here, just as He did in Luke 24:49.

For John truly baptized with water; but ye shall be baptized with the Holy Ghost not many days hence. Acts 1:5

In the Book of Acts, Jesus explained that the Promise was the baptism of the Holy Ghost. Did not God the Father give Jesus power according to John 17:2, so that Christ could give eternal life?

As thou hast given him power over all flesh, that he should give eternal life to as many as thou hast given him. John 17:2

This power is mentioned in Acts.

But ye shall receive power, after that the Holy Ghost is come upon you: and ye shall be witnesses unto me both in

ETERNAL LIFE BY WAY OF JESUS

*Jerusalem, and in all Judaea, and in Samaria, and unto
the uttermost part of the earth. Acts 1:8*

Jesus told the disciples that they would receive power after the Holy Ghost would come upon them. And He formerly said that the Father gave Him power so that Jesus could give the disciples eternal life. With this in mind, consider the following point:

Jesus said the Father gave Him power, and He was then to give the disciples eternal life.

Jesus indeed explained that the disciples would receive power when they would receive the Holy Ghost.

These two points lead to the single conclusion that the eternal life He would give them is the power of the Holy Spirit – the very Life essence of the Fruit of the Tree of Life!

And it is the promise of the Father, since Jesus took it from the Father and gave it in turn to the disciples. It is God's eternal life. Receiving God's Spirit is receiving God's eternal Life! It is taking a bite of eternal life!

Now, Jesus told the disciples in Luke 24 to preach the message of repentance and remission of sins in His name. And they were told to begin to do so in Jerusalem.

*But ye shall receive power, after that the Holy Ghost is
come upon you: and ye shall be witnesses unto me both in
Jerusalem, and in all Judaea, and in Samaria, and unto
the uttermost part of the earth. Acts 1:8*

TAKE A BITE OF ETERNAL LIFE

The command to begin to preach to all nations in Jerusalem is repeated in Acts 1:8 above. Jerusalem was mentioned first. This tells us that nobody had yet preached this message. Not even Jesus had preached this message! It was to be preached beginning in Jerusalem after Jesus ascended. Then Jesus was said to have left the world. Reading down through Acts Chapter One we read:

> *Then returned they unto Jerusalem from the mount called Olivet, which is from Jerusalem a Sabbath day's journey. Acts 1:12*

So they went to Jerusalem, where they would begin to preach the message commanded of Jesus. Nobody on earth heard anybody preach this message up until this time. Jesus told the Disciples to begin preaching a message after He died, was buried, resurrected, and lived 40 days in His resurrected body that nobody had ever preached before! In fact it was not until ten more days after He ascended that they indeed did preach this message for the very first time. In total, over 50 days passed from the day Jesus told the penitent thief he could enter paradise until the message to be preached to all nations was first preached. They could not preach this message until they received the promise of the Father – the Holy Ghost.

While waiting in Jerusalem for the power of the Holy Ghost, the promise, we read this of the disciples...

> *And suddenly there came a sound from heaven as of a rushing mighty wind, and it filled all the house where they were sitting. And there appeared unto them cloven tongues like as of fire, and it sat upon each of them. And*

64

> *they were all filled with the Holy Ghost, and began to*
> *speak with other tongues, as the Spirit gave them*
> *utterance. Acts 2:2-4*

They got the power! They bit into the fruit of Life and received eternal life. In Matthew 28:19 we saw that all power (represented by the Lamb's seven horns) was given to Him. And we now discover that Jesus gave power to the disciples. And He had all wisdom (seven eyes) and abounded in wisdom towards us (for our sakes!) by revealing it to us! Also note that when Jesus uttered the truth that all power was His, he then proceeded to tell the disciples to baptize people in the Name.

Recall that Jesus had not yet died and had not yet given the disciples eternal life in John 17:1-3. He said, "As thou hast given him power over all flesh, that he should give eternal life to as many as thou hast given him." The phrase "that he should give," relates to us He did not yet provide anybody with life yet. Instead He planned to do so at that time. When did He give that eternal life?

> *He that believeth on me, as the scripture hath said, out of*
> *his belly shall flow rivers of living water. (But this spake*
> *he of the Spirit, which they that believe on him should*
> *receive: for the Holy Ghost was not yet given; because that*
> *Jesus was not yet glorified.) John 7:38-39*

After He died and was glorified, He gave this eternal life. After the lamb died and rose again to take the book, we read that He told John to take it and eat the book. And then He told John to prophesy. In Luke 24, Jesus told them to begin preaching the message of repentance and remission of sins in

His name at Jerusalem. But He said they must tarry in Jerusalem until they were endued with power from on high before they would begin to preach that message.

And, behold, I send the promise of my Father upon you: but tarry ye in the city of Jerusalem, until ye be endued with power from on high. Luke 24:49

We found that power to be distinctly called the Baptism of the Holy Spirit. They returned to Jerusalem not yet having preached to anybody, for they were told to wait there until they were endued with power from on high. They had not received the Holy Spirit yet! So they waited. And while they waited, they received the power! The Holy Ghost filled them! They were then ready to start preaching this great message for the first time in history!

People from all over Jerusalem came to find what happened to these people once it was noised abroad. Peter told them about Jesus' death and how that God raised Him up. Upon hearing this, the people asked Peter a question that prompted him to preach, for the first time, the very thing Jesus commanded the disciples to preach after they were endued with power.

Now when they heard this, they were pricked in their heart, and said unto Peter and to the rest of the apostles, Men and brethren, what shall we do? Then Peter said unto them, Repent, and be baptized every one of you in the name of Jesus Christ for the remission of sins, and ye shall receive the gift of the Holy Ghost. Acts 2:37-38

ETERNAL LIFE BY WAY OF JESUS

He did it! He preached the message! Jesus told him to preach repentance! Peter said, "Repent!" Jesus told him to preach "remission of sins in His name", and Peter told them they would receive remission of sins in Jesus' name through baptism!

> *...be baptized every one of you in the name of Jesus Christ for the remission of sins.*

In other words, Peter, like John in the Book of Revelation, ate the book and received eternal life when he received the baptism of the Holy Ghost. And then he prophesied to "many nations," beginning at Jerusalem.

Praise the Lord! It is so clear! The Word has always been known to be our provision of eternal Life. Jesus told us to eat His flesh and drink His blood to receive eternal life. He is the Word made flesh. He referred to His words as being our source of eternal life when he told us to eat His flesh.

> *It is the spirit that quickeneth; the flesh profiteth nothing: the words that I speak unto you, they are spirit, and they are life. John 6:63*

Can you catch the pattern in the Word of God represented as the fruit of eternal life today? And can you see this same image found in the picture of Jesus plucking the book from God's hand and giving it to John that he might eat it? Revelation is speaking of a judgment of God, and John preached about such judgment. But the pattern in reading of his prophecy to all nations, after having eaten the book, clearly shows us that the Book with which John was empowered with eternal life contained the message John had to preach to all nations.

ALL POWER IN THE BLOOD (7 HORNS OF THE LAMB)

Jesus had seven horns, indicating all power. We must recognize that this power points to the blood He shed and offered in the heavenly holiest of holies. The Lamb had seven horns. The Lamb had all power. That was particularly noted when John heard the multitude praise Him for redeeming them by His blood.

In Israel's entry into Canaan following Joshua, the first campaign against an enemy was at the battle of Jericho. The people marched around the city for six days. On the seventh day they were told to march around it seven times, and seven priests were to blow seven trumpets made from ram's horns.

> *And seven priests shall bear before the ark seven trumpets of rams' horns: and the seventh day ye shall compass the city seven times, and the priests shall blow with the trumpets. And it shall come to pass, that when they make a long blast with the ram's horn, and when ye hear the sound of the trumpet, all the people shall shout with a great shout; and the wall of the city shall fall down flat, and the people shall ascend up every man straight before him. Joshua 6:4-5*

The picture we see in the blowing of a trumpet represents the preaching of the Word.

ETERNAL LIFE BY WAY OF JESUS

Cry aloud, spare not, lift up thy voice like a trumpet, and shew my people... Isaiah 58:1

It even gives the hint of revelation. "Shew my people..." What message can we get from the blowing of seven ram's horns for the destruction of Jericho? What truth can there be other than the message of the power of the blood of Jesus being proclaimed against any enemy or fortress that hinders our walk?

As we have noted, seven signifies the thought of being "complete" and "all". Seven horns represent all power. The insight the story Jericho offers into this picture, with the blowing of seven ram's horns, is the thought of preaching the almighty power of the blood of Jesus. It was the blood of Jesus that broke the devil's hold on our lives. It was the blood that washed away our sins and paid the price of redemption. It was the blood of Jesus Christ that paved the way back into the Garden as a kind of Red Carpet for us to enter upon. Jesus gave us the Red Carpet Treatment!

As Christians, we are to come into a place of great faith and victory and power. Israel's entrance into Canaan, after having been bound as slaves in Egypt, foreshadows the entrance of a believer into a place of dominion in which God initially created Adam to live! Whatever resistance you face on your way into the Garden Throne-room with the Lord, your promised land of dominion, you must speak the word of faith. This Word bases your surety of victory against the enemy upon the blood of Jesus Christ. Blow the 7 trumpets! Speak the whole truth!

TAKE A BITE OF ETERNAL LIFE

So many people are in need of more complete revelation of the power of the blood. The church requires ministers who know the absolute power of the blood, that they might preach it and show God's people. It is interesting that after noticing the seven trumpets, made from seven ram's horns, we see Jesus as a lamb with seven horns. We then read of seven trumpets that are sounded later in the Book of Revelation. Clearly these trumpets are made from the seven horns of the lamb!

Jesus secured the world for His Kingdom the day He presented the Blood. Yet it is not until the seventh trumpet that we read the following:

> *But in the days of the voice of the seventh angel, when he shall begin to sound, the mystery of God should be finished, as he hath declared to his servants the prophets. Revelation 10:7*

> *And the seventh angel sounded; and there were great voices in heaven, saying, The kingdoms of this world are become the kingdoms of our Lord, and of his Christ; and he shall reign for ever and ever. Revelation 11:15*

The sounding of the seven trumpets indicates that the message of the blood of Christ, and all its power, must be preached in entirety to the saint of God. The saint of God must receive a full revelation of the blood's power. Until one fully (-7-) understands the power of the blood, one will not enjoy the victory Christ paid for so long ago!

Are you weak and lukewarm, with little victory in your Christian walk? It is because there is the need of receiving a fuller revelation of the power of the blood of Jesus Christ. Jesus' blood not only redeemed us from sin, but it also is our basis for daily strength in the midst of trials and opposition from the enemy. When we speak the word of faith against the enemy and wickedness, we speak it "in Jesus' Name." Many do not understand the need to verbally invoke "Jesus' name". Reference to His Name in such an invocation is meant to express faith in the power of the blood that Jesus shed for us on the cross as our authority for demanding evil to fall down flat before our feet.

We must understand that we have been given power against the enemy and we are to rule as kings and priests in life over our circumstances right now! Paul said we are "more than conquerors". No human word can describe the power we possess in Jesus' name, and so all that Paul could say was "more than conquerors"! Jesus, the Son of God, went to the Ancient of Days and took dominion and power for us that we might reign on the earth. This is talking about power in the here and now.

CANAAN AND THE GARDEN OF EDEN

Many feel Canaan represents Heaven, and in one sense it may. However, I read of no giants and well-walled cities in Heaven that we must tear down and conquer. Canaan can be seen to represent the Garden of Eden. When Israel entered Canaan, the enemy was not going to leave without a fight. God instructed Israel to blow seven trumpets made from ram's horns and watch the walls of Jericho fall flat. So must we enter our places in the Garden of the Kingdom of God and sound out the word of faith and authority by the almighty

71

blood of Jesus Christ. The blood is our ticket to glory and our means of authority against all enemies.

When the saint of God receives a full understanding of the power he/she possesses due to the blood of Jesus, then the saying of Revelation 11:15 can individually be fully enjoyed:

> *And the seventh angel sounded; and there were great voices in heaven, saying, The kingdoms of this world are become the kingdoms of our Lord, and of his Christ; and he shall reign for ever and ever. Revelation 11:15*

Some are yet in the first trumpet stage and are not fully aware of the message of truth. They doubt much. But they are on their way to all (7) truth! They will soon hear the seventh trumpet and enjoy personal victory. Seven trumpets mean all truth.

> *Howbeit when he, the Spirit of truth, is come, he will guide you into all truth: for he shall not speak of himself; but whatsoever he shall hear, that shall he speak: and he will shew you things to come. John 16:13*

During the seven trumpets, we read that many earth-shaking events occur. I feel these apply to troubles in the physical world, during the wrath of God. However, let us take note that this can be applied to our personal lives, and that is what this book is concerned with. Our personal worlds, where sin and doubt try to bring us down, are to be judged and rendered ineffective against our spiritual progress. As we more perfectly (7) understand the word of truth concerning the power of the Blood towards us, our personal worlds of trial and pressure from the enemy will be dealt with in increasing victory. And when we fully appreciate the power towards us in the Blood, our entire worlds (our flesh was made from the dust of the earth) – our very lives – will be ruled by Jesus Christ and we shall rule our lives with Him.

Paul said just that in his letter to the Romans regarding Jesus' redemption since Adam's failure:

> *For if by one man's offence death reigned by one; much more they which receive abundance of grace and of the gift of righteousness shall reign in life by one, Jesus Christ.)* Romans 5:17

The Kingdoms of our hearts are fully ruled by Christ when we fully comprehend the glory He gave to us when He redeemed us, and we reign in life with Him. Who would not render all to Him after they learn of such liberty He paid for?

So, child of God, speak the truth of the all powerful blood of Jesus as your authority against all resistance on your way towards all of God's promises for your life!

6

TWELVE MANNER OF FRUIT

In the midst of the street of it, and on either side of the river, was there the tree of life, which bare twelve manner of fruits, and yielded her fruit every month: and the leaves of the tree were for the healing of the nations.
Revelation 22:2

When John saw the New Heaven and New Earth, He saw the New City with a river and the Tree of Life beside it. That Tree is the same one mentioned in Genesis 2. On that tree were twelve manners of fruit. I see a connection to the twelve apostles who helped comprise the foundation of the Church. Keep in mind that Jesus told the disciples to wait for the promise of the Holy Ghost in Jerusalem and then to begin preaching to all nations. Judas was dead and gone, and another had to be chosen to see twelve there in Jerusalem to receive this power. We can see the reason for the twelve fruit on the tree (in the City New Jerusalem). The twelve fruit represented the twelve Apostles' doctrine. This reminds me of the twelve baskets of bread fragments carried by the twelve apostles after the Lord fed the five thousand. It speaks of the eternal Spirit of Life, plus the thought of doctrine. Was it not a book which John ate? "Doctrinal truths"? "Words of God"? Did not Jesus say, "My doctrine is not mine, but his that sent me." (John

74

7:16), indicating the Father gave him the fruit/revelation, and Jesus had to give eternal life to His servants, the disciples (John 17:2; Revelation 1:1)?

The leaves on the Tree of Life were for the "healing of the nations." In other words, "John, take and eat and preach to all nations."

In the prayer about those whom the Father gave to him (John 17:2), Jesus referred to the 12 apostles.

> *For I have given unto them the words which thou gavest me; and they have received them, and have known surely that I came out from thee, and they have believed that thou didst send me. I pray for them: I pray not for the world, but for them which thou hast given me; for they are thine. John 17:8*

> *Neither pray I for these alone, but for them also which shall believe on me through their word; John 17:20*

Jesus said that He gave his servants, the twelve apostles, the words that can very correctly be called the words of eternal life, in view of John 17:2, and prayed for the people who would believe upon Jesus through the apostles' word! After Peter initially preached that word commanded by Jesus before He left, we read:

> *And they continued stedfastly in the apostles' doctrine and fellowship, and in breaking of bread, and in prayers. Acts 2:42*

75

TAKE A BITE OF ETERNAL LIFE

The twelve apostles' doctrine is represented by the twelve fruit of life on the tree for all nations. The apostles preached the word to all nations.

> *...These that have turned the world upside down are come hither also; Acts 17:6*

Revelation 7 recounts that people from all nations heard the doctrine of eternal life, and stand on the sea of glass by the throne unhindered from entrance by the four Beasts, when all were formerly barred from that sea before the throne in Revelation Chapter 4!

And in this passage we see a beautiful picture of man back in the Garden with the Tree of Life, represented by the throne of God, about which were four Beasts who formerly kept man out.

> *After this I beheld, and, lo, a great multitude, which no man could number, of all nations, and kindreds, and people, and tongues, stood before the throne, and before the Lamb, clothed with white robes, and palms in their hands; And cried with a loud voice, saying, Salvation to our God which sitteth upon the throne, and unto the Lamb. And all the angels stood round about the throne, and about the elders and the four Beasts, and fell before the throne on their faces, and worshipped God, Saying, Amen: Blessing, and glory, and wisdom, and thanksgiving, and honour, and power, and might, be unto our God for ever and ever. Amen. Revelation 7:9-12*

The reason we see the throne of God with one sitting in it before Jesus redeemed us, is due to the fact that two were meant to be seated there. Adam should have ruled with God, but he fell. Only God sat there in the throne meant for Himself and Adam. However...

> *To him that overcometh will I grant to sit with me in my throne, even as I also overcame, and am set down with my Father in his throne. Revelation 3:21*

Once again mankind will reign with Christ as Adam should have reigned with God on His throne. Oh, there is not a gigantic throne with a million seats for us to sit on beside God. God is an omnipresent Spirit and is unlimited to space. The throne is symbolic of the dominion Adam originally had and lost.

As we close this chapter, read once again the words of the Beasts who formerly blocked man from the Garden as they praise God for Jesus' redemption!

> *And when he had taken the book, the four Beasts and four and twenty elders fell down before the Lamb, having every one of them harps, and golden vials full of odours, which are the prayers of saints. And they sung a new song, saying, Thou art worthy to take the book, and to open the seals thereof: for thou wast slain, and hast redeemed us to God by thy blood out of every kindred, and tongue, and people, and nation; And hast made us unto our God kings and priests: and we shall reign on the earth. And I beheld, and I heard the voice of many angels round about the throne and the Beasts and the elders: and the number of them was ten thousand times ten thousand, and thousands of thousands; Saying with a loud voice, Worthy is the Lamb that was slain to receive*

power, and riches, and wisdom, and strength, and honour, and glory, and blessing. And every creature which is in heaven, and on the earth, and under the earth, and such as are in the sea, and all that are in them, heard I saying, Blessing, and honour, and glory, and power, be unto him that sitteth upon the throne, and unto the Lamb for ever and ever. And the four Beasts said, Amen. And the four and twenty elders fell down and worshipped him that liveth for ever and ever. Revelation 5:8-14

7

THE FOUR RIVERS OF EDEN

There is a river, the streams whereof shall make glad the city of God, the holy place of the Tabernacles of the most High. Psalm 46:4

The Psalm described the manner in which God's Spirit moves through His people today, to flow forth from our lives in power and energy. Power of God's Spirit is transformed in believers' lives to come forth differently than it first enters our lives. Human Beings were created to be *transformers*, taking intangible glory from God and changing it into physical power and ministry for the lives of those in this world who need God.

Similarly, the single River of Life entered the Garden and there was transformed and turned into four rivers.

And a river went out of Eden to water the garden; and from thence it was parted, and became into four heads. (11) The name of the first is Pison: that is it which compasseth the whole land of Havilah, where there is gold; (12) And the gold of that land is good: there is bdellium and the onyx stone. (13) And the name of the second river is Gihon: the same is it that compasseth the whole land of Ethiopia. (14) And the name of the third river is Hiddekel: that is it which goeth toward the east of

79

TAKE A BITE OF ETERNAL LIFE

Assyria. And the fourth river is Euphrates. (15) And
the LORD God took the man, and put him into the
garden of Eden to dress it and to keep it.
Genesis 2:10-15

There a single river from which several streams go forth
and gladden the City of God. What a wonderful parallel to
the river of Eden! The four rivers are the streams in the
Psalm that leave the Garden, (the Garden is the counterpart
to the City New Jerusalem), and reach the whole world.

There is a message: When the church of God, His people, are doing their part in labouring for His cause by watching and praying, like Adam's task of keeping and dressing, the
outward flow of the Spirit is maintained.

The River represents the flow of the Spirit of God
through His Church.

When we fulfill our part for Him, oh, how we, the City
of God, are glad! Nothing is more fulfilling than accomplish-
ing our destined purpose. All mankind is destined to be
God's transformers in this world.

Notice how the Psalm also speaks of the Tabernacles of
the Most High. The Tabernacle, Garden and New City all
stand for the same thought of God's junction place in this
world – The Church! We will speak of this later in more detail.

Jesus worked in another Garden, Gethsemane, and acted
as the Last Adam who dressed and kept the Garden. That is
why we read that He "sweat" blood. Sweat indicates work.

The type of work He did was intercessory work, for the behalf of lost humanity, through self-denial. He was a transforming station, literally a power house, to convey and produce the will of God in this world.

The workers in any power station must maintain their efforts of efficiency so that the current of electricity continues to flow to the world and enlighten the darkness and make life more comfortable. We, too, must maintain our work in dressing and keeping this Garden. This will allow the power of the Spirit to work in us that we might witness of Jesus Christ, the light of the world, the power of God, to lost humanity.

Names are provided for us describing these four rivers of Eden, and are specified from first to last in a particular sequence in the Bible. This is given to us for a special reason. These rivers are given a specific priority in relation to one another by being referred to as the "first river", "second river", "third river", and "fourth river". Why? God has a reason for everything He does.

The Lord simply does not provide information in the Bible so as to merely satisfy man's curiosity of how man began, and inform us of the origin of our creation just to let us know where we came from. The Bible concerns itself with much more important issues for salvation and God's plan for mankind. This tells us that the Bible accounts, even concerning even such seemingly trivial things as the naming of four rivers, have something to do with salvation for mankind.

God has a message for us concerning the ministry of His Spirit, and of certain priorities we must keep in mind in this list of names. We must look at these rivers, the details of their descriptions, and pray for illumination about the message the Lord wants us to learn

THE FOUR RIVERS NAMED

The name of the first is Pison: that is it which compasseth the whole land of Havilah, where there is gold; And the gold of that land is good: there is bdellium and the onyx stone. And the name of the second river is Gihon: the same is it that compasseth the whole land of Ethiopia. And the name of the third river is Hiddekel: that is it which goeth toward the east of Assyria. And the fourth river is Euphrates. Genesis 2:11-14

PISON: The name Pison is translated as increase. It is derived from the thought of spreading, growing up, and grown fat. Dispersive is the point. God's first and foremost priority in the thought of having His Spirit flow through us to the world is the idea that it must be dispersed. As much of the dry world as possible must be saturated with the Spirit of God! This must be our first priority after receiving God's Spirit. Jesus said it was given to us as Power to witness! We must understand that we are not to reserve this living water up for ourselves, but to shed it forth for others. God's Spirit will not sit still and stagnate!

GIHON: The name Gihon means *bursting forth*! Hallelujah! Can you see the second priority of the Spirit? The name Gihon is derived from the idea of coming forth, taking, and bringing forth. It implies the idea to burst forth.

82

Once we understand that the Spirit must flow forth from our lives, our second priority is to ensure that when it flows out it must always flow bountifully, bursting forth from our lives. We are not meant to merely trickle forth the Spirit of God, like a weak creek with hardly any flow at all. We must be filled with the Spirit so that it overflows forth everywhere around us!

HIDDEKEL: The third river was called Hiddekel. It means *rapid*. The thought of a *sharp voice* is also associated with the meaning of this name. Our third priority in working with the Spirit is the thought of a quick work that God desires to accomplish through us, and we must clearly sound the truth as we let the Spirit flow through us.

EUPHRATES: The final river is called Euphrates. It implies *fruitfulness*. Is not this the end result of the flowing of God's Spirit in proper ministry as it is meant to flow through us? The land will be fruitful, if we maintain the former three priorities.

THE SANCTITY OF THE GARDEN

This precious Junction point for the River must be protected from corruption of fleshliness and worldliness. That is the reason Adam was to keep (or protect) the Garden. If Satan managed to invade the Garden, he would have opportunity to stop the flow of the pure Spirit of Life to the entire lost world. The Garden had to remain holy! And from our text, we find that the streams from the river make glad the City, the holy place of God.

Immediately after reading of the four rivers, we read that God put man in that junction point.

By reading the account in this order, it was as though God emphasized to us that this place was a very special place. After reading of all these details of the very names of the rivers, we read man was specifically put *there* by God. God had a particular interest in mind when he put man in that Garden. It had something to do with these rivers. It is noteworthy that God went into great detail describing the region and the river, including their names, and then tell us that He put man in that very location where the river divided into four.

And the LORD God took the man, and put him into the Garden of Eden to dress it and to keep it. Genesis 2:15

God previously planted the Garden eastward in Eden. He caused a River to flow from Eden onward into this Garden that it might water the paradise prepared for man. From that point, the river would, in turn, separate into four other rivers.

The name Eden actually means Paradise. We can therefore consider Eden to be the Paradise of God about which we read in the New Testament. Jesus told the penitent thief that he would be with Him in Paradise on that very day of their deaths. Jesus referred to what we commonly call Heaven after the thief asked the Lord to remember him in His Kingdom.

Paul also wrote of Paradise when he shared his experience of having been caught up to hear unspeakable words that were not lawful for a man to utter. Again, we understand this to be Heaven.

Not only is Eden referred to in God's creation, but a Garden is also noted as being eastward in Eden (Genesis 2:8). It is commonly mistaken today that the Garden was Eden, but the Bible specifically tells us that it was eastward *in Eden*. Eden was a larger district surrounding the Garden. God planted the Garden eastward in that region of Eden. This, too, is very notable, as we shall see.

This entire story about the Garden has great meaning for us today in our Christian walks.

THE KINGDOM OF GOD

God made Adam from the dust of the ground and afterwards placed man in that Garden. Note that man was not made from the dust of the Garden. He was made outside of the Garden, and afterwards placed within it.

As Adam was placed in the Garden of Eden, we were placed within the Kingdom of God upon new birth. Jesus told Nicodemus that one must be born of water and Spirit to enter the Kingdom. A kingdom is naturally understood to be ruled by a King. Since Adam was to reign the world from that position in the Garden, we can understand how the Garden represented the Kingdom of God from which the believer rules.

Jesus said the Kingdom is within you (Luke 17:21).

TAKE A BITE OF ETERNAL LIFE

Paul spoke of the world of the Holy Ghost when he said the kingdom of God is not meat and drink (Romans 14:17). The Church comprises God's Kingdom, and Adam represents those who are put within the Kingdom of God.

Luke chapter 3 lists Adam in a genealogy of Christ as a "son of God," obviously since he had no earthly father. Sons of God rule, or are intended to rule. Notice the following verse in respect of this thought:

> *Who hath delivered us from the power of darkness, and hath translated us into the kingdom of his dear Son: Colossians 1:13*

We were put into the Kingdom of God where Jesus rules, as Adam was put into his Kingdom in the Garden.

As Adam was filled with God's breath of life, we were filled with God's Spirit when God readied us for entrance into the Kingdom of God. God took us out from the dust and dirt of this world and filled us with His Spirit, and then placed us in His Kingdom.

> *And the LORD God formed man of the dust of the ground, and breathed into his nostrils the breath of life; and man became a living soul. Genesis 2:7*

> *And when he had said this, he breathed on them, and saith unto them, Receive ye the Holy Ghost: John 20:22*

> *And suddenly there came a sound from heaven as of a rushing mighty wind, and it filled all the house where they were sitting. And there appeared unto them cloven*

86

tongues like as of fire, and it sat upon each of them. And they were all filled with the Holy Ghost, and began to speak with other tongues, as the Spirit gave them utterance. Acts 2:2-4

God breathed His breath into those in the upper Room on the day of Pentecost as they were filled with the Holy Ghost.

8

GO WEST, YOUNG MAN!

The Garden was eastward in Eden. In order to appreciate the point of this eastward position we must consider the events involving *compass points* later in the Eden story. The bible often makes mention of something to set the stage for what we shall read about later. In this case, not only was the Garden eastward in Eden, but this direction is again mentioned in regards to one of the two sons whom Adam fathered. After man was cast out of the Garden, Cain and Abel were born. Cain murdered his brother, Abel, and was sent by God into the land of Nod. Nod was located *east* of Eden (Genesis 4:16).

Get the picture. The Garden was in Eden, and specifically in the eastward part of that region of Eden. Nod was even further east still, outside of Eden altogether. The direction of the east is mentioned several times in this single story of Adam and Eve. God planted the Garden *eastward* in Eden (Genesis 2:8). He placed Cherubims and a flaming sword at the *east* of the Garden when he expelled man from it (Genesis 3:24). Cain went *east* of Eden into the land of Nod (Genesis 4:16).

Anyone who reads and studies the Bible will notice a pattern of the association of certain thoughts with important

88

points in every instance those points are mentioned in scripture. For instance, many times in Scripture we read about the
compass points of east and west in relation to God's people
and error. When Lot departed from Abraham, into his back-
slidden condition toward Sodom and Gomorrah, he went
eastward, as did Cain (Genesis 13:11). After Israel completed
the Exodus, the Reubenites requested to be positioned in the
wilderness east of Jordan and not in the land itself (Jo-
shua.13:8; Joshua18:7; 1 Chronicles 6:78).

The east direction always seemed to involve the idea of
the direction away from the will of God. Reuben's heritage
was foretold by his father, and it was a bad one (Genesis 9:3-
4). So, it is no wonder that the Reubenites chose to stay in
the wilderness, eastward of the Land, rather than possess the
land which God promised them, typical of their failing position with God. The heritage of Reuben in the light of his err-
ing ways was fulfilled in the tribe after his name. Reuben did
not desire the things which God planned for Israel. History
tells us that the land outside of Israel, in which Reuben chose
to dwell, was overtaken by others, and in time nomadic people dwelt there. Reuben lost his region – it came to pass that
he simply did not excel.

We also find that the evil city Babylon was built in an
eastward location according to Genesis 11:2-4.

All evil things were seemingly located eastward of God's
appointed territories, and evil people in scripture journeyed
away from God, as it were, to the east.

GO WEST, YOUNG MAN

Eden was the territory of God's people, and it represents the Heavenly things. The Garden of God's territory was eastward in Eden. All of this forms into a spiritual direction in which Cain journeyed in relation to that which represents Heavenly things. Just as Cain went eastward into the land of Nod and fathered his lineage there, apart from the Garden, we see a spiritual picture of unsaved humanity. Spiritually speaking, man is born outside of Eden in the land of wandering, for Nod literally means "wandering and unrest". As Israel traveled westward over Jordan in order to enter Canaan, we see that the westward direction represents spiritual progress towards God's will.

If we are all spiritually born in the *east*, outside of the Garden, we see a picture of the positioning of the Garden between lost humanity and Eden. In other words, the Church, or the Garden, is the closest thing to Heaven! We must travel, as it were, westward, into the Kingdom within the Church. To get to Heaven, we must go through the Church!

As the settlers in the days of early America used to say, we must, "Go west, young man!"

Scripture tells us that Jesus would travel westward, as the lightning shines from the east to the west (Matthew 24:27).

Both the Tabernacle and Temple each had only one entrance that was located in the east of the structures. In order to enter into the structure, one had to travel westward. In that manner a person would approach the presence of God located in the inner sanctum of the holy building called the Holiest of Holies. This is identical to the lay-out of the Garden of Eden where Cherubims were placed at the east entrance to the Garden! The only reason God would bar the east end of the Garden could only be due to the fact that the one and only entrance was located there. Otherwise, He would have placed flaming swords and Cherubims around the full circumference of the Garden.

If you look closely, you find there are many, many likenesses between the Temple and the Garden.

HELP IS NEEDED EASTWARD

The relationship that Adam enjoyed with the very Presence of God itself was experienced in the Garden of Eden. As Adam was evicted from the Garden premises, mankind has been born in a separated state from God due to his sin. So we could say that a spiritual description of man's return to this joyous intended fellowship with God would be a journey back into the Garden. If the world in sin is represented as being eastward, we can readily see pictures in the Bible that indicate help for those who are in the east that they might be saved and come back to God's fellowship once again.

Israel wandered (the meaning of "Nod") through the wilderness on their way to Canaan, spiritually representing man's need to return to the Garden.

They wandered in the wilderness in a solitary way; they found no city to dwell in. Psalm 107:4

91

Recall that Abraham was originally taken to that that land after he left Ur of the Chaldees. Later, his descendants, Jacob and the eleven patriarchs, left Canaan and traveled down into Egypt. There, Joseph dwelt in rulership during the famine. They left the Promised Land! They were outside of the place God intended them to be. Israel had to later return there, just as man left the Garden of fellowship with God due to sin and must return in salvation today!

Although Egypt is west of Israel, the journey that ended their trek in the wilderness caused them to stand in need of crossing the Jordan River in a westward direction, as though they went beneath the promised land and back up and around in order to enter it *from the east* (Joshua 5:1; 12:7 – the "other side of Jordan," outside the Land, was said to be eastward in Joshua 12:1).

DRY PLACES

Spiritually speaking, humanity exists eastward. This direction indicates the idea of being lost and of wandering. In the wandering desert we find that Israel dwelt in a dry place. Jesus said that demon spirits lurk in the dry places when cast out of a person. Jesus, Himself, had to walk through the dry wilderness for forty days and then be tempted of the devil in that dry wilderness, as though the devil abides in such places.

> *When the unclean spirit is gone out of a man, he walketh through dry places, seeking rest, and findeth none.*
> *Matthew 12:43*

Moses struck the rock, and waters of life were said to specifically flow in the dry desert places!

GO WEST, YOUNG MAN!

He opened the rock, and the waters gushed out; they ran in the dry places like a river. Psalm 105:41

Christ is that Rock (1Cor 10:4). As the Rock gave forth waters for life, Jesus said we would receive eternal life if we would eat His flesh and drink His blood (John 6:53-55).

The disciples heard this and were confused as to what He meant by eating his physical flesh. Did He actually propose cannibalism? Jesus sensed their confusion, and explained that He was not literally referring to flesh. He was speaking spiritually. He was the Word made flesh. His flesh represented His words that were the true source of Spirit and Life.

It is the spirit that quickeneth; the flesh profiteth nothing: the words that I speak unto you, they are spirit, and they are life. John 6:63

Recall that the Word of God is quick (Hebrews 4:12), or "alive". Jesus' words were Spirit and they "quickeneth"-or make alive. But this is not any ordinary Life, though! It is eternal Life. He is the Rock from which His blood and Spirit flow into the dry places like a river (Psalm 105:41). It is the true river of life. And we drink of it!

Many abandoned Jesus after He made this speech that day. He then asked the disciples if they would also depart from Him. The multitude only came to see miracles, and revealed they cared less for His teaching. Notice how His disciples responded about His words.

93

TAKE A BITE OF ETERNAL LIFE

Then Simon Peter answered him, Lord, to whom shall we
go? thou hast the words of eternal life. John 6:68

Peter understood what he meant by eating flesh and
drinking blood. He realized Christ referred to His *Words* that
give life and are Spirit. Peter could never depart from Jesus,
since he fully understood that Jesus was the only source for
the words that grant a person eternal life when they are *eaten*,
or believed.

Thank God for the river of life in His blood. His blood
contains the New Testament, or, in other words, it contains
His Word for us today from God. Can you see the link between the blood of Jesus, the Word of God and the River of
Life?

Likewise also the cup after supper, saying, This cup is the
new testament in my blood, which is shed for you.
Luke 22:20

THE END OF WANDERING IN DRY PLACES: THE JORDAN

Jordan River is a spiritual symbol that marks the end of
wandering and the beginning of life in the Garden. When
Jesus was baptized, it was the day He entered the wilderness
to be tempted of the devil. The devil roamed in the realm of
the dry place of the wilderness, which typically speaks of the
dry places where the living water of the Spirit is absent. (We
know the devil is not restricted to physically dry places,
though, of course. It's the symbol involved in a dry desert
place, spiritually devoid of Life).

94

GO WEST, YOUNG MAN!

Notice Jesus was baptized in Jordan. As Israel had to cross westward over Jordan in order to enter the Land, Jesus went in the reverse direction and departed from Israel crossing Jordan eastward into the wilderness. Spiritually, the directions represent how He left the realm of Heaven (Eden) eastward after His baptism, and entered a physical place that represented lost humanity's domain – the wilderness of wandering. He went to the place where we spiritually were – in the wilderness and dry places. There He experienced all the temptations we face, and He overcame them all as He began His ministry!

Please understand that Adam was thrust eastward out of the Garden when he fell. All man is born in sin and, as it were, eastward of the Garden. The entire coming and purpose for the ministry of the Son of God can be understood as we picture God having come down from Heaven to be incarnated as a man. In that incarnation He figuratively walked eastward over Jordan to the abode of sin in which we were born. Since Adam failed, and thrust us all Eastward into sin, Jesus, the Last Adam, indicated His journey's purpose to free us from sin by having walked eastward out of Israel to the desert to retrieve us. There Jesus overcame that which bound us – the devil and sin. (No man can lead anybody else through a victory through which He has not already proven Himself victorious. Therefore, Jesus, Himself, first had to walk into that dry place and overcome before He could minister to us.)

In His crossing into the wilderness through Jordan, we see more than just a picture of a physical direction in which He walked. There is a picture of God coming to rescue us from wandering.

9

GOD IS THE DELIVERER

Israel followed a pillar of fire and cloud towards Canaan. From this we can perceive that we will not wander in Nod if we would only follow Christ's direction and leading.

> They wandered in the wilderness in a solitary way; they found no city to dwell in. Hungry and thirsty, their soul fainted in them. Then they cried unto the LORD in their trouble, and He delivered them out of their distresses. And he led them forth by the right way, that they might go to a city of habitation. Psalm 107:4-7

He delivered them and He led them.

Moses first tried to deliver Israel by fighting Egypt, after having killed an Egyptian who beat a Hebrew slave. He discovered that fighting is not God's plan. God's plan is *deliverance*. There is a big difference between fighting something and delivering people from it. When Moses met God at the burning bush, God corrected the prophet and showed him that it was not that Moses was intended to fight Egypt, but that God would deliver Israel out of Egypt. So many times we try to fight the enemy, when we've already been delivered by God from him!

96

THE INCORRECT MANNER IN WHICH
TO DEAL WITH FLESH

Today, too many believers actually fight their own flesh
and try to coerce it to do good in order to be the proper
Christians they know they should be. Like Moses, they are
mistaken, though they are very sincere.

Paul attempted to fight his own flesh with his frail human efforts, as follows:

> *I find then a law, that, when I would do good, evil is
> present with me. For I delight in the law of God after the
> inward man: But I see another law in my members,
> warring against the law of my mind, and bringing me into
> captivity to the law of sin which is in my members.*
> *Romans 7:21-23*

He explained that he learned from experience how a believer will fail and be made captive in a far worse degree than
was already experienced, if such a believer tries to fight the
tendencies of the flesh in his/her own power in order to live
righteously! It is not that we should fight, but rather that
God must deliver. Paul discovered the very thing Moses
learned at the burning bush:

> *And the LORD said, I have surely seen the affliction of
> my people which are in Egypt, and have heard their cry by
> reason of their taskmasters; for I know their sorrows;
> And I am come down to deliver them out of the hand of
> the Egyptians, and to bring them up out of that land unto
> a good land and a large, unto a land flowing with milk
> and honey; unto the place of the Canaanites, and the*

Hittites, and the Amorites, and the Perizzites, and the Hivites, and the Jebusites. Exodus 3:7-8

O wretched man that I am! Who shall deliver me from the body of this death? I thank God through Jesus Christ our Lord. So then with the mind I myself serve the law of God; but with the flesh the law of sin. Romans 7:24-25

Who will deliver? The answer: God will! Paul thanked God that He would do it, and he said the manner in which God would deliver him was through Jesus Christ.

The phrase "through Jesus Christ" actually means "by virtue of the work Jesus did in shedding His blood in sacrifice," or, "by virtue of the river of Life, His blood", the greatest provision Jesus ever provided for humanity! It means, "Not by human might, nor human power," as Paul taught, but "by God's Spirit" (Zech. 4:6)!

Jesus delivers us as the pillar of fire delivered Israel from Egypt by leading them.

My sheep hear my voice, and I know them, and they follow me: John 10:27

Jesus saith unto him, If I will that he tarry till I come, what is that to thee? follow thou me. John 21:22

Having this idea of following our shepherd, Jesus, in mind, notice:

The LORD is my shepherd; I shall not want. He maketh me to lie down in green pastures: he leadeth me

beside the still waters. He restoreth my soul: he leadeth
me in the paths of righteousness for his name's sake.
Psalm 23:1-3

He is the Light! He is clothed with a cloud! He is the
pillar of cloud and fire that led Israel through the dry wilderness! He leads us out of the wilderness into the Garden!
Paths of righteousness are the way of the Tree of Life, mentioned at the end of the Garden story.

When the High Priest entered the Most Holy place of
the Tabernacle and Temple, he sprinkled the blood of the
atoning sacrifice on the *east* part of the Ark of the Covenant's
lid, the mercyseat (Leviticus 16:14). This also gives us the
beautiful truth that Christ, who is the great High Priest, died
for lost humanity where they wander eastward in the dry
places of sin. He shed His blood for those in the dry places.
His river of Life flowed eastward!

Notice in Revelation that the River flows from the
throne. The true fountain of eternal youth – Jesus' blood –
flows for our eternal life!

And he shewed me a pure river of water of life, clear as
crystal, proceeding out of the throne of God and of the
Lamb. Revelation 22:1

We read above about "...the throne of God and the
Lamb!" Why is it a throne of both God and the Lamb? It is
because God delivered us through Christ. Praise God!

Ministry must be accomplished eastward. All of lost
Humanity is eastward. This river flowed eastward from Eden

99

into the Garden, and, in turn, branched out into four rivers that left the east entrance of the Garden to the entire world. We see a symbolic message here of how the Spirit of God reaches outward in ministry to lost humanity.

Four rivers leave the east region of Eden, and proceed from there to all the rest of the world. This tells us that the whole world is figuratively eastward, compared to Heaven, and wandering in sin.

10

THE RIVER OF THE SPIRIT

As the River of Eden flowed into the Garden from Eden/Paradise, the Spirit of God descended from Heaven, or from Paradise. What a wonderful parallel!

And the Holy Ghost descended in a bodily shape like a dove upon him, and a voice came from heaven, which said, Thou art my beloved Son; in thee I am well pleased.
Luke 3:22

The Spirit descended from Heaven (the true Eden) above. Another point to notice is the manner in which Jesus likened the Spirit of God to living water. The River of Eden was the River of Life.

Jesus answered and said unto her, If thou knewest the gift of God, and who it is that saith to thee, Give me to drink; thou wouldest have asked of him, and he would have given thee living water. John 4:10

But whosoever drinketh of the water that I shall give him shall never thirst; but the water that I shall give him shall be in him a well of water springing up into everlasting life. John 4:14

TAKE A BITE OF ETERNAL LIFE

He that believeth on me, as the scripture hath said, out of his belly shall flow rivers of living water. (But this spake he of the Spirit, which they that believe on him should receive: for the Holy Ghost was not yet given; because that Jesus was not yet glorified.) John 7:38-39

One day, in a vision, God pointed Ezekiel to the River of God's Spirit which flowed eastward, exactly as the River of Eden flowed into the Garden!

Then brought he me out of the way of the gate northward, and led me about the way without unto the utter gate by the way that looketh eastward; and, behold, there ran out waters on the right side. And when the man that had the line in his hand went forth eastward, he measured a thousand cubits, and he brought me through the waters; the waters were to the ankles. Afterward he measured a thousand; and it was a river that I could not pass over: for the waters were risen, waters to swim in, a river that could not be passed over. Ezekiel 47:2-5

Then said he unto me, These waters issue out toward the east country, and go down into the desert, and go into the sea: which being brought forth into the sea, the waters shall be healed. And it shall come to pass, that every thing that liveth, which moveth, whithersoever the rivers shall come, shall live: and there shall be a very great multitude of fish, because these waters shall come thither: for they shall be healed; and every thing shall live whither the river cometh. And it shall come to pass, that the fishers shall stand upon it from Engedi even unto Eneglaim; they shall be a place to spread forth nets; their fish shall be according to their kinds, as the fish of the great sea, exceeding many. Ezekiel 47:8-10

Though this passage regards certain specific prophetic truths, we still can glean a beautiful general picture of God's Spirit from it. His Spirit travels eastward into the dry places of the world, where God's Spirit is not known. Multitudes of fish, representing the souls of men for whom we must become fishers, are found and freed from the wandering in the seas of life wherever the Spirit flows. Jesus told us to be fishers of men. We depend upon the Spirit in our efforts to win souls, as the fishermen stood upon the river. Without the strengthening and anointing of the Spirit of God as our basis for ministry, we simply cannot adequately minister to lost humanity.

Ezekiel saw another vision depicting dryness and spiritual saturation of Life:

The hand of the LORD was upon me, and carried me out in the spirit of the LORD, and set me down in the midst of the valley which was full of bones, And caused me to pass by them round about: and, behold, there were very many in the open valley; and, lo, they were very dry. Ezekiel 37:1-2

The dry bones came together by the word of God:

So I prophesied as I was commanded: and as I prophesied, there was a noise, and behold a shaking, and the bones came together, bone to his bone. And when I beheld, lo, the sinews and the flesh came up upon them,

and the skin covered them above: but there was no breath
in them. Ezekiel 37:7-8

But it also took something more than Word. Spirit was
required, just as Adam was made from the dust of the earth
and required the breath of the life of God's Spirit to then enter into him afterwards. There is more God has for us than
simply listening to the preached Word of God. There is the
Holy Spirit baptism!

Then said he unto me, Prophesy unto the wind, prophesy,
son of man, and say to the wind, Thus saith the Lord
GOD; Come from the four winds, O breath, and breathe
upon these slain, that they may live. Ezekiel 37:9

Four Winds! Like the Four Rivers of Eden. Recall the
day of Pentecost when a mighty rushing wind filled the house
as the one hundred and twenty believers were filled with the
Holy Ghost!

Therefore prophesy and say unto them, Thus saith the
Lord GOD; Behold, O my people, I will open your
graves, and cause you to come up out your graves, and
bring you into the land of Israel. Ezekiel 37:12

The Jews were to return to their land as all of mankind
must spiritually return to the Garden of Eden. The Holy
Ghost brings us into the Garden! It brings us in to the Kingdom of God. We can be born of the water and of the Spirit
in order to enter the Kingdom, or into the Garden, and rule!

THE RIVER OF THE SPIRIT

Jesus answered, Verily, verily, I say unto thee, Except a man be born of water and of the Spirit, he cannot enter into the kingdom of God. John 3:5

Since blood is the Life of the flesh (Leviticus 17:11), we can also see this picture of the River of Life in the blood which the High Priest sprinkled eastward in the Tabernacle.

It is noteworthy that the evil spirits cast out of people go into dry places. Spirits of Satan hate God's Spirit and His Presence. The Spirit of God is like a River. And if anything typically represents the abode of evil spirits, it would be a desert and dry place, void of the wetness of the Spirit.

Creatures of darkness and desert life are used to describe evil spirits in the words which God gave concerning Idumea, figuratively the enemies of the Church.

And thorns shall come up in her palaces, nettles and brambles in the fortresses thereof: and it shall be an habitation of dragons, and a court for owls. The wild Beasts of the desert shall also meet with the wild Beasts of the island, and the satyr shall cry to his fellow; the screech owl also shall rest there, and find for herself a place of rest. There shall the great owl make her nest, and lay, and hatch, and gather under her shadow: there shall the vultures also be gathered, every one with her mate. Isaiah 34:13-15

We need to saturate this dry, old world with God's living water of Spirit and drive out all evil spirits wherever they may lurk!

The woman at the well met Jesus and thirsted for water in a very spiritual manner, for she lived in sin and in a spiritual dry place for many years. Thank God for the Living Waters of Life!

JUNCTION POINT OF THE SPIRIT

If the Spirit is pictured as flowing from Eden in the form of a River, towards and into the Garden of the Church, and branching into four more rivers at this Garden, we see that the Garden is a sort of junction point. The four rivers leave the Garden and go into four more regions. The number 4 seems to often be associated with the idea of something about the world. Four Gospels are written, Matthew, Mark, Luke and John, for the world to hear and be saved. Often we read of the four corners of the earth. The inhabitants of the world are described in four consecutive terms: Every kindred, and tongue, and people, and nation (Revelation 5:9). Judgments against man are pictured as four: The sword, judgment, or pestilence, or famine (2 Chronicles 20:9), "...my four sore judgments... the sword, and the famine, and the noisome Beast, and the pestilence," (Ezekiel 14:21).

So we can see that the four rivers leaving the Garden speak of the Spirit of God reaching in ministry out to all the four corners of the world from the Church! We truly must understand this reason as to why the Spirit is within us.

The Upper Room can also be considered a kind of Garden into which God's Spirit descended as a mighty river of wind from the origin of Heaven. At that point in the world, in the Garden of the Upper Room in Jerusalem, Jesus specifically directed the believers to wait. As with the picture of the

106

Garden's junction point, from the Upper Room in Jerusalem they would minister to four listed points. And the same passage tells us why the River of Spirit is given to us:

> *But ye shall receive power, after that the Holy Ghost is come upon you: and ye shall be witnesses unto me both in...*
>
> *1) Jerusalem,...*
> *2) and in all Judaea,...*
> *3) and in Samaria,...*
> *4) and unto the uttermost part of the earth. — Acts 1:8*

The Spirit is given to us as power in order to be able to witness. Witness is ministry to the world. We must witness of Christ's resurrection and salvation to the world in sin. From the Upper Room, where the saints first received the Spirit of power, they were to go out into the whole world (indicated by the four regions mentioned).

Before the day of His crucifixion, Jesus prayed in a Garden (Gethsemane), and His blood, His very Life, sweat out through His flesh. He prayed in this sweating manner for lost humanity, and for the death He had to experience on the cross for mankind. A river of life flowed in a Garden for the entire world of lost humanity.

He *sweat forth* His blood! Sweat depicts work. Jesus had a job to do! Adam's task was to dress and keep the Garden. Jesus had to watch and pray!

WORK AT THE JUNCTION POINT

And the LORD God took the man, and put him into the Garden of Eden to dress it and to keep it. Genesis 2:15

Since the River's junction point between God and the world was situated in the Garden, these two efforts of dressing and keeping, reserved for Adam's work, were most important! The River flowed in a pure form into the Garden, and had to remain pure in order for it to reach its destination and accomplish a work. Wherever the River would flow, fruitfulness and life would flourish. God desired the Garden to spread, as it were, across the face of the world. It would broaden and increase its boundaries due to the fruitfulness that the four rivers would provide to the outside regions. That is part of the reason God placed man in the Garden.

Should the River be cut off, the fruitfulness would cease spreading outward to the world, and dryness of sin and evil would remain.

We cannot allow ourselves to be contaminated with fleshliness and thus corrupt the unadulterated ministry of the Spirit through us to the world! We must maintain our purity in Christ, so that we, in turn, may dress and keep the Garden. This would allow the River to remain pure that it may reach the world in purity.

Our enemy had to find a way into the Garden to stop this work of God. He subtly chose to enter the serpent, a creature of the field (not of the Garden), in order to gain that entrance. If Satan could stop man from dressing the Garden (building it up and outward), and keeping the Garden (protecting its sanctity for the River's sake), the devil could rule earth instead of this "son of God," Adam (Luke 3:38). The devil could then render the earth into a huge, dry and devastated desert, rather than a fruitful Garden. He would turn earth into another void and wasted *moon* if he could.

So, the picture of four rivers leaving the Garden tell us of the Spirit of God transformed into active ministry in the Garden/Church from which it will leave and minister to the whole world.

Ministry of the Spirit, whether it be in preaching, healing, or a word of encouragement at the right time, is that which was formerly incorporeal and intangible and *non-relative* to the world, and translated into activity and physical working that humanity can relate to. The world cannot see nor hear God. But we can! Therefore, we are a junction point.

The Church is a vital place in the plan of God. It is strategically located between heaven and the world of lost souls. It is a transformation centre into which the Spirit of God to be transformed into ministry in the physical. The Church is the Temple of the Holy Ghost where man meets God. The Church is the Body of Christ. With our regenerated spirits, we are the contact point between lost humanity and God. We can hear God, whereas the world is deaf to His voice. And unless God can use us to minister in this world, the message for them will never reach them.

We are like a hydro-electric power plant where water flow is transformed into power to enlighten the dark world!

TAKE A BITE OF ETERNAL LIFE

Jonah was told to go to Ninevah and preach judgment of God to the people there. Why did not God speak directly to Ninevah, Himself? Ninevah was unable to hear God's voice. No wonder God took Jonah through such awful lessons in order for him to obey God and go to Ninevah!

Without us, Church, the world will be lost without hope. We are the salt of the earth.

God placed Adam in a very important location in the world – the most important place in the world.

Since the River of Life was to flow into the entire world, the junction point determined the preservation of its purity. You see, evil was in the world. A corruptive element was already at work when God placed Adam in the world. Satan was out there. That is the reason God put Adam in the Garden to dress and to keep it. Keeping the Garden means protecting it and preserving it "as is". The evil outside the Garden was the element which God wanted to remain outside the Garden. And Adam's job was to do just that. Keep it outside.

By dressing and Keeping the Garden, Adam would maintain his position of rulership under God.

And God said, Let us make man in our image, after our likeness: and let them have dominion over the fish of the sea, and over the fowl of the air, and over the cattle, and over all the earth, and over every creeping thing that creepeth upon the earth. Genesis 1:26

THE RIVER OF THE SPIRIT

The work of dressing and keeping is a work in which all believers must labour. Jesus likewise told the disciples in the Garden of Gethsemane to do two things that night in the Garden – Watch and Pray. Watching is keeping or protecting. Praying is dressing.

We must dress this Garden and maintain its beauty and build it up and increase its borders. Prayer maintains our relationship with God and enhances our spirituality so that our effectiveness in ministering to this lost world may be maintained at a maximum potential.

Watching is keeping a look-out while we work for God, that we do not become infected by lies from the devil. We must keep the world out of our lives and out of our Garden. If the corruption from the world enters our lives, and we are adulterated from the purity of union with God alone, the work of the Spirit in us will be tainted with fleshliness and worldliness. This will cause us to exude an impure work of God to the world. Flesh will be mingled with our ministries, and a distortion of God's Will is then manifested to humanity.

When Nehemiah restored the walls of Jerusalem, his men did two things which also represent our need to watch and pray. They worked with a building tool in order to build up the walls with one hand, and held a weapon in the other, watching. Jerusalem also represents the Garden!

And it came to pass from that time forth, that the half of my servants wrought in the work, and the other half of them held both the spears, the shields, and the bows, and the habergeons; and the rulers were behind all the house of

111

Judah. They which builded on the wall, and they that bare burdens, with those that laded, every one with one of his hands wrought in the work, and with the other hand held a weapon. For the builders, every one had his sword girded by his side, and so builded. And he that sounded the trumpet was by me. And I said unto the nobles, and to the rulers, and to the rest of the people, The work is great and large, and we are separated upon the wall, one far from another. In what place therefore ye hear the sound of the trumpet, resort ye thither unto us: our God shall fight for us. So we laboured in the work: and half of them held the spears from the rising of the morning till the stars appeared. Nehemiah 4:16-21

DENY SELF

Since the blood represents the Life of the flesh (Leviticus 17:10-11) we can see that Jesus taught us a lesson when He shed His blood by sweating it forth as He prayed in the Garden. We already noted how sweat indicates work and exertion. In sweating blood, Jesus showed how we must deny ourselves since blood is the life of our own flesh. Self-denial is the work we must accomplish that the Spirit might ever flow from the church like a river! Our Lives must be lost in exchange for His life. It is not our wills, but His will that we must fulfill.

Then said Jesus unto his disciples, If any man will come after me, let him deny himself, and take up his cross, and follow me. For whosoever will save his life shall lose it: and whosoever will lose his life for my sake shall find it. Matthew 16:24-25

112

THE RIVER OF THE SPIRIT

We must labour in the Garden, as did Adam, and deny ourselves to let the Spirit flow outward.

Verily, verily, I say unto you, Except a corn of wheat fall into the ground and die, it abideth alone: but if die, it bringeth forth much fruit. He that loveth his life shall lose it; and he that hateth his life in this world shall keep it unto life eternal. John 12:24-25

The above verses in John's Gospel first speak about a kernel of wheat falling into the ground and dying. Look at the corn of wheat as life encased in a shell. Unless that shell is broken by falling into the ground and thereby deteriorating, the life cannot come forth and multiply itself. So must we deny our lives, or the shell of the natural and the carnal, in order for God's Spirit within to flow out of us and out to the dry world as a River of Life! Hallelujah!

Perhaps the River was cut off when Adam fell from the Garden. One never knows. At any rate, God will cut off the flow of the Spirit into our lives if we do not remain pure. He does not want His Spirit corrupted by fleshliness in His desires to minister that Spirit outward to lost humanity through us.

Since God chose to flow through us by way of His Spirit, we must accept our responsibility of remaining sensitive to His voice through prayer, and remaining pure for His use through watching.

Nevertheless, Satan did indeed enter the Garden and lied to Eve. God previously told Adam, "Of every tree of the Garden thou mayest freely eat: But of the Tree of the Knowledge of Good and Evil, thou shalt not eat of it: for in the day that thou eatest thereof thou shalt surely die" (Genesis 2:16-17). Then the devil said, "Ye shall not surely die" (Genesis 3:4).

A lie felled Eve, and she succumbed to the temptation and committed sin. In turn, she urged Adam to sin and he, too, fell. Both were cast outward to the east territory away from the Garden.

The junction point was corrupted.

SATAN ENTERS ANOTHER GARDEN

The Garden of Gethsemane was again invaded by the devil millennia after Satan possessed the serpent. This time he possessed Judas. In that manner he entered the Garden to attempt to take down the Son of God, the Last Adam, as he did the first Adam.

Before all of this, when Jesus spoke of the Life in His Blood, we read that He immediately thought about Judas. Perhaps Jesus had the River of life in mind, and how the devil possessed the serpent and corrupted the purity of the Garden.

It is the spirit that quickeneth; the flesh profiteth nothing: the words that I speak unto you, they are spirit, and they are life. But there are some of you that believe not. For Jesus knew from the beginning who they were that believed not, and who should betray him. John 6:63-64

Likewise also the cup after supper, saying, This cup is the new testament in my blood, which is shed for you. But, behold, the hand of him that betrayeth me is with me on the table. Luke 22:20-21

The very same devil that possessed the serpent in Eden also entered into Judas!

Then entered Satan into Judas surnamed Iscariot, being of the number of the twelve. Luke 22:3

Satan recognized Jesus as the Last Adam, and tried to repeat his efforts which succeeded in Eden so long ago.

As the serpent used its mouth to speak forth a lie to Eve, Judas betrayed Jesus with a kiss of his mouth (perhaps intended to deceive the second Eve, the disciples who stood nearby and were the then-future church). Praise the Lord that He did not fall as Adam did, but went all the way to the cross despite the shame and agony.

11

THE END, AND A RETURN
TO THE GARDEN

The picture of the Tree of Life and the River of Eden is seen again in the end of the Bible in Revelation. The Tree and the River are there in the new City, New Jerusalem, as they were in the Garden of Eden. And the city comes down to earth, where the Garden originally was.

> *And he shewed me a pure river of water of life, clear as crystal, proceeding out of the throne of God and of the Lamb. In the midst of the street of it, and on either side of the river, was there the tree of life, which bare twelve manner of fruits, and yielded her fruit every month: and the leaves of the tree were for the healing of the nations.*
> *Revelation 22:1-2*

The River is clear as crystal. Pure.

Note the preceding verse to this passage as follows:

> *And there shall in no wise enter into it any thing that defileth, neither whatsoever worketh abomination, or*

maketh a lie : but they which are written in the Lamb's book of life. Revelation 21:27

Speaking of the New City, we are told that nothing unclean can enter the City should it defile the City. And it specifically points to the very thing that caused the River of Eden to be contaminated in Genesis, as it lists all that which is barred from the City – "Whatsoever... maketh a lie." A lie felled mankind and corrupted the River, in a sense. It is a lie that is specifically noted as being one of the elements which are barred from ever entering that New City. All is restored as it was in Genesis, only the Garden will be replaced by the progressive phase of a City. The Garden City! The thought is that God's original intent was for Adam to dress the Garden and build it up into a City with all his descendants living in that great paradise of the Garden. How else would Adam and his children dwell in the Garden together? This, of course, though, was thwarted by Adam's sin.

Recall that Abraham looked for a City as he journeyed into the land of Canaan, which typified the Garden. In fact, the spies called the Land one that *flowed with milk and honey*. A Garden, so to speak!

THE TREE OF LIFE

The River in the New City is as clear as crystal. It is pure. This water feeds the tree of Life, since it watered the Garden, according to Genesis:

> *And a river went out of Eden to water the Garden; and from thence it was parted, and became into four heads. Genesis 2:10*

117

TAKE A BITE OF ETERNAL LIFE

As the River watered the Garden, it watered the Tree of Life. The eternal Life from the Tree's fruit was meant to be received by man, but without the River of Life watering that tree we see that the fruit would never have been manifested for man's benefit.

Jesus is the fruit of Life on the Tree. Although the Cross was a tree of death for Him, it became a Tree of Life for you and me! Thank God!

> *Then Jesus said unto them, Verily, verily, I say unto you, Except ye eat the flesh of the Son of man, and drink his blood, ye have no life in you. Whoso eateth my flesh, and drinketh my blood, hath eternal life; and I will raise him up at the last day. John 6:53-54*

Since He is the Word made flesh, we can readily apply John 6:53-54 to believing Jesus' Words. It's not the literal Body of Jesus to which He referred, but the Words He spoke.

> *It is the spirit that quickeneth; the flesh profiteth nothing: the words that I speak unto you, they are spirit, and they are life. John 6:63*

> *Then Simon Peter answered him, Lord, to whom shall we go? thou hast the words of eternal life. John 6:68*

Leaves are for shelter, covering and comfort, as are wings in scripture. We read of the leaves of the tree of life as being for the purpose of healing the nations. With the troubles of sin and iniquity having been around since Adam's fall, there is much healing required for all the nations.

THE END, AND A RETURN TO THE GARDEN

In the midst of the street of it, and on either side of the river, was there the tree of life, which bare twelve manner of fruits, and yielded her fruit every month: and the leaves of the tree were for the healing of the nations. Revelation 22:2

Jesus is like the fruit on the Tree of Life and also the leaves. The Tree of life was anointed by the River of Life, the Spirit, for the distinct purpose, among others, of healing:

The Spirit of the Lord is upon me, because he hath anointed me to preach the gospel to the poor; he hath sent me to heal the brokenhearted, to preach deliverance to the captives, and recovering of sight to the blind, to set at liberty them that are bruised, Luke 4:18

Jesus is the sun of righteousness, for healing:

But unto you that fear my name shall the Sun of righteousness arise with healing in his wings; and ye shall go forth, and grow up as calves of the stall. Malachi 4:2

Wings, like leaves, are used to indicate the thought of protection and shelter – Luke 13:34. The Spirit of God anointed Jesus to heal, as the River of Life watered the tree of life that its leaves might heal the nations. A curse does not exist any in the City, as opposed to the curse that was first introduced in the Garden.

And there shall be no more curse: but the throne of God and of the Lamb shall be in it; and his servants shall serve him: Revelation 22:3

119

THE CHURCH TODAY

What might have occurred with mankind in relation to the Garden had Adam not fallen? Keep in mind that it was a holy place, where God's very presence walked with Adam. He would have remained as High Priest, in a sense, while He ruled the world under God, for Jesus, the Last Adam, was High Priest. Of course, Adam would not have offered a blood sacrifice, for blood was only for the remission of sins, and there would have been no sin had Adam not fallen. Nevertheless, it seems that all Adam's descendants would have gathered to the Garden and regularly partook of the fruit of the Tree of Life as Adam led the people in worship. Or perhaps the Garden would have expanded across the earth. At any rate, the fruit of the tree of Life would have been man's food.

Well, this did not occur, but in a sense it is occurring through another means – the Church. The Church is the spiritual Garden. It is like living in a paradise with God to be born again and in the Church – the true Church! What a life! The preaching of the cross is the Tree of Life in the form of words that offer fruit of Life. Jesus' words are fruit of eternal life to those who come to the Body of the Church to hear and believe them.

Could the purpose of the River of the Spirit, branching out and reaching all of the world, also be present to attract people to the source of that River – the Garden, that they might also become part if it?

We have been given Jesus' holiness. All that we can do in the form of works is to keep it. We cannot attain it, nor work to get it, but we can work to keep it. Adam could not create the Garden, but simply kept it, or protected it.

The New Jerusalem forms the continuance of the intended story of the garden, after that story was interrupted by man's sin. Let us not fail as did Adam.

12

THE FOUR WINDS OF HEAVEN

Let us consider the Cherubims again more closely. God has some incredible truths contained in the pictures of Cherubims for us to understand in regards to our authority and power as His people. As we have seen, Cherubims are noted from Genesis to Revelation. They are part of the great and overall plan of the ages in the Church. They were first mentioned at the fall of Adam as Guardians placed in the entrance to the Garden, and they are again noted in Revelation as four Beasts. Suffice it to say, their role in the Bible is very significant.

Many people commonly misunderstand the concept of any form of Prophecy to be the foretelling of future events – future prediction alone. Technically speaking, "prophecy" in itself is simply the anointed, inspired utterances of any of God's truths. Prophecies may regard future predictions, and they may not. However, *predictive* prophecy alone is relegated to the foretelling of events to come, while *prophecy* in general is simply the inspired speaking of God's word.

This is important to know since John's conversation with an angel in his visions of Revelation informs us that the "spirit of prophecy is the testimony of Jesus."

The spirit of a thing is its very source and essence. It is its reason for being and is the inspiration for its very existence. So, the very inspiration of prophecy lends itself to the essence of all Jesus taught, and all that Jesus did for us in this world – that being His testimony. The very Gospel message can actually be called the Testimony of Jesus!

Christ once said that no one comes to the Father but through Him. This is precisely what is meant by saying all prophetic, inspired speaking of God's word is rooted in nothing less than the testimony of Jesus Christ. Christ is the only way to God and even to the truths of God. Everything focuses around Christ in all of God's inspired words to mankind. This is one reason why the third chapter of 2 Corinthians teaches us how a veil remains over one's heart who refuses to learn of the New Covenant and remain in the Old, disabling one from truly seeing God's glory until one turns that heart to Jesus. Even when Jews remain beneath the Old Covenant and study Moses' Law, they will never truly understand that law until they turn their hearts to Jesus Christ. Only then can God remove the veil form their understanding.

FOUR BEASTS

Revelation chapter 4 reads of four Beasts that were depicted as having the appearance of specific creatures. Note:

> *And before the throne there was a sea of glass like unto crystal: and in the midst of the throne, and round about the throne, were four Beasts full of eyes before and behind. And the first Beast was like a lion, and the second Beast like a calf, and the third Beast had a face as a man, and the fourth Beast was like a flying eagle. Revelation 4:6-7*

123

TAKE A BITE OF ETERNAL LIFE

1. The FIRST BEAST was described as a LION.

2. The SECOND BEAST was a CALF, or YOUNG OX.

3. The THIRD BEAST was a MAN.

4. The FOURTH BEAST was an EAGLE.

They are listed in this order for a good reason, as were the four rivers in Genesis 2. Later in the book of Revelation we see reference to "the second Beast," and the "third Beast," etc., without an explicit statement as to which Beast is which. So the listing and the numbering of the Beasts in chapter 4 are intended to be kept in mind. (You will find that every single detail and word written in Revelation is there for a very good reason!)

Furthermore, these faces are not alien to the rest of the Bible. Ezekiel recounts the vision of Cherubims with these very faces, letting us know the Beasts of Revelation are indeed the Cherubims of Ezekiel's vision!

Also out of the midst thereof came the likeness of four living creatures. And this was their appearance; they had the likeness of a man. And every one had four faces, and every one had four wings. And their feet were straight feet; and the sole of their feet was like the sole of a calf's foot: and they sparkled like the colour of burnished brass. And they had the hands of a man under their wings on their four sides; and they four had their faces and their wings. Their wings were joined one to another; they turned not when they went; they went every one straight forward. As for the likeness of their faces, they four had

THE FOUR WINDS OF HEAVEN

the face of a man, and the face of a lion, on the right side:
and they four had the face of an ox on the left side; they
four also had the face of an eagle. Ezekiel 1:5-10

Ezekiel did not see a UFO, as some have imaginative
folks have proposed. He saw a vision of symbolic elements.
He saw four living creatures and called the same creatures
"Cherubims" in Ezekiel 10:1.

Picture this representation in the following diagram:

Notice that Ezekiel saw the particular faces in specific locations in relation to one another. The first face he mentioned was the man's face on the Cherubims. You could say that the frontal aspect of each of the four beings had the man's likeness. Then he saw the ox on the left side, the lion is on the right side and finally he described the face of the eagle. The face of the eagle was, therefore, situated at the rear position of the quartet of heads, while the prophet faced the likeness of the man. This is notable, for it corresponds to other elements in the Bible. Let me mention again that every point mentioned in God's Word is very important and should not be overlooked.

These same four faces are depicted upon the standards of the four camps that encamped about the Tabernacle when it was pitched in wilderness journeys, as found in Numbers chapter two. Observe the layout of the camps in relation to the Tabernacle itself. Each of the twelve tribes was situated under one of four tribal standards.

Those four tribal standards, beneath which the four groups were stationed, were Judah, Ephraim, Dan and Reuben.

Judah's emblem was the Lion, emblazoned on Judah's standard. This group was situated east of the erected Tabernacle (Numbers 2:3). Three of twelve of the tribes ranked themselves beneath this standard at the east of the Tabernacle.

Reuben's standard portrayed the image of a man, and this group pitched south of the Tabernacle (Numbers 2:10).

Ephraim's emblem was the young ox, and pitched west of the Tabernacle (Numbers 2:18).

Finally, Dan was represented by the eagle, and pitched north of the camp (Numbers 2:25).

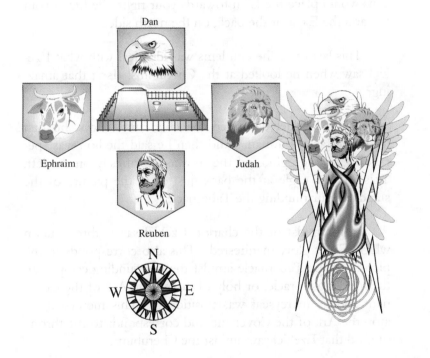

Dan

Ephraim

Judah

Reuben

N
W   E
S

These correspond perfectly with the position of the four faces on each Cherub in Ezekiel's vision! The Tabernacle entrance always faced the East direction when it was erected. This meant that each of the four sides of the Tabernacle always faced the same compass direction, and always corresponded with the same standard emblems of the four tribes. Therefore, if you were *positioned at the south* of the Tabernacle and faced northward, Reuben's standard of the man's face would be positioned directly in front of you every time you faced north towards the Tabernacle whenever it was erected. This would place the Lion towards your right, the Ox at your left and the Eagle at the back, on the north side.

This layout of the emblems was identical with what Ezekiel saw when he looked at the Cherubims! Isn't that amazing?

When Ezekiel described the cherubim's faces, he first listed the face of a man. And then he said the lion was specifically on the right, and the ox was specifically on the left. This left the eagle at the back, just as in the picture of the standards surrounding the Tabernacle.

In the midst of the chariot, Ezekiel saw a throne upon which God's glory manifested. This also corresponds to the picture of the Tabernacle amidst the surrounding camps. In the innermost oracle, or holy of holies, the Ark of the Covenant and its mercyseat was positioned. This mercyseat sat atop the Ark of the Covenant, and corresponds to the throne of God that Ezekiel saw amidst the Cherubims.

> *And above the firmament that was over their heads was the likeness of a throne, as the appearance of a sapphire stone: and upon the likeness of the throne was the likeness as the appearance of a man above upon it. And I saw as the colour of amber, as the appearance of fire round about within it, from the appearance of his loins*

even upward, and from the appearance of his loins even downward, I saw as it were the appearance of fire, and it had brightness round about. As the appearance of the bow that is in the cloud in the day of rain, so was the appearance of the brightness round about. This was the appearance of the likeness of the glory of the LORD. And when I saw it, I fell upon my face, and I heard a voice of one that spake. Ezekiel 1:26-28

Keep in mind that the standards were positioned around that focal point in the same positions every time the people set up camp.

The chariot Ezekiel saw was said to not turn, as it were. "It turned not." In other words, if the chariot was moving in a particular direction, and began to veer off towards another compass point, it did not wholly swerve towards that direction and then head there. When driving a car, we would turn the vehicle and the entire body of the vehicle would change positions and head into the direction in which we desired to go. This was not the case with the chariot. Ezekiel noted that the chariot had wheels within wheels that somehow allowed the chariot to go in any direction simply by the Spirit directing the wheels to turn in their proper manner, so as to leave the body of the chariot always facing the same direction, while the wheels alone accordingly spun to change the vehicle's direction of travel.

> *The appearance of the wheels and their work was like unto the colour of a beryl: and they four had one likeness: and their appearance and their work was as it were a wheel in the middle of a wheel. When they went, they went upon their four sides: and they turned not when they went. Ezekiel 1:16-17*

One could picture each of the wheels as being comprised of two. There was a wheel within the middle of a wheel. They would appear as the four wheels of a cart, but would each contain a second wheel pointed in a perpendicular fashion within the first. It would therefore work in similar fashion to a cart with swiveling wheels that could be moved around in any direction without rotating the actual body of the cart.

> *Thus were their faces: and their wings were stretched upward; two wings of every one were joined one to another, and two covered their bodies. And they went every one straight forward: whither the spirit was to go, they went; and they turned not when they went. Ezekiel 1:11-12*

The creatures, then, would not turn as they went. They always faced one direction no matter if they actually went in another direction. This allowed the four faces of the Cherubims to maintain their positions in respect to the compass points with the lion always to the right, or east, and the ox to the left, or west, etc. This brings us to an amazing conclusion! The chariots and the faces of the Cherubims correspond perfectly to the demand for the Hebrews to position the camps of Israel under the same four standards in the same four compass positions! This is surely beyond coincidence, and shows us the singular thread of a thought throughout the entire Bible regarding the Cherubims. What is God trying to tell us?

We see the four Beasts again in Revelation Chapter 6. They are each associated with one of the four horses of the apocalypse and their riders. John saw white, red, black and pale horses.

Now, consider the vocabulary in the following verses:

THE FIRST BEAST

And I saw when the Lamb opened one of the seals, and I heard, as it were the noise of thunder, one of the four Beasts saying, Come and see. And I saw, and behold a white horse: and he that sat on him had a bow; and a crown was given unto him: and he went forth conquering, and to conquer. Revelation 6:1-2

The first Beast mentioned in Revelation 4:7 was the lion. Recall that Judah's banner matched this Beast's likeness and was positioned east of the Tabernacle in Numbers Chapter 2. And the first horse was white. The white horse corresponds to the Lion's face, and for a particular reason. You might notice that we do not specifically read that the Lion was the Beast who told John to see the white horse. We only read, "One of the four Beasts." However, the remaining three horses were associated with particular Beasts/Cherubims, and this brings us to understand the Beast in verse 1 was indeed the Lion.

THE SECOND BEAST

And when he had opened the second seal, I heard the second Beast say, Come and see. And there went out another horse that was red: and power was given to him that sat thereon to take peace from the earth, and that they should kill one another: and there was given unto him a great sword. Revelation 6:3-4

We distinctly read the "second Beast" spoke to John to see the red horse. According to Revelation 4:7, the "second Beast" is listed as the Calf, or Ox. And the Calf was portrayed upon Ephraim's standard, situated west of the Tabernacle. The corresponding horse was red.

THE THIRD BEAST

And when he had opened the third seal, I heard the third Beast say, Come and see. And I beheld, and lo a black horse; and he that sat on him had a pair of balances in his hand. And I heard a voice in the midst of the four Beasts say, A measure of wheat for a penny, and three measures of barley for a penny; and see thou hurt not the oil and the wine. Revelation 6:5-6

When we turn to Revelation 4:7, we find the third Beast to be the image of a man in appearance, and it corresponded with the black horse of famine.

THE FOURTH BEAST

And when he had opened the fourth seal, I heard the voice of the fourth Beast say, Come and see. And I looked, and behold a pale horse: and his name that sat on him was Death, and Hell followed with him. And power was given unto them over the fourth part of the earth, to kill with sword, and with hunger, and with death, and with the Beasts of the earth. Revelation 6:7-8

The fourth Beast was the eagle, and this standard was positioned north in the camps. It corresponded with the pale horse of death and hell.

In summary:

TAKE A BITE OF ETERNAL LIFE

LION is associated with the WHITE HORSE

OX-RED HORSE

MAN-BLACK HORSE

EAGLE-PALE HORSE

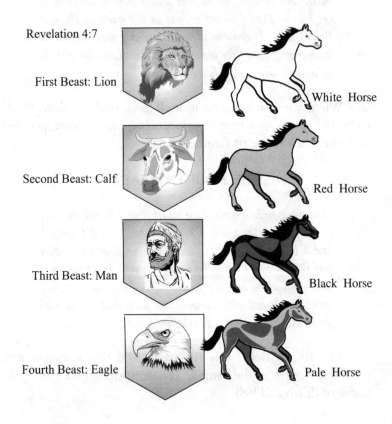

Revelation 4:7

First Beast: Lion — White Horse

Second Beast: Calf — Red Horse

Third Beast: Man — Black Horse

Fourth Beast: Eagle — Pale Horse

THE FOUR WINDS OF HEAVEN

Combine this thought with the compass positions in which the four Beasts or Cherubims were positioned.

LION EAST OF TABERNACLE associated with the WHITE HORSE

OX WEST OF TABERNACLE associated with the RED HORSE

MAN SOUTH OF TABERNACLE associated with the BLACK HORSE

EAGLE NORTH OF TABERNACLE associated with the PALE HORSE

Picture the compass points:

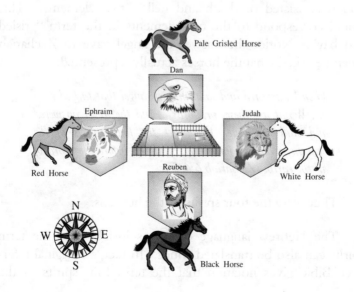

ZECHARIAH'S VISION OF THE HORSES

Zechariah saw a vision of the four horses also. And in his vision, compass points were specifically noted!

And I turned, and lifted up mine eyes, and looked, and, behold, there came four chariots out from between two mountains; and the mountains were mountains of brass. In the first chariot were red horses; and in the second chariot black horses; And in the third chariot white horses; and in the fourth chariot grisled and bay horses. Zechariah 6:1-3

These same coloured horses of Revelation 6 are mentioned above in Zechariah 6. The grisled and bay would be another term for the pale horse. The pale horse of Revelation 6 consisted of death and hell – two elements. This would correspond to the two elements in the term "grisled and bay". Notice the answer the angel gave to Zechariah when he asked what the horses actually represented:

Then I answered and said unto the angel that talked with me, What are these, my lord? And the angel answered and said unto me, These are the four spirits of the heavens, which go forth from standing before the Lord of all the earth. Zechariah 6:4-5

They were the four spirits of the heavens.

The Hebrew language offers us insight that the term spirits can also be translated winds. In fact, a marginal reference Bible gives notation that the term four spirits of the

THE FOUR WINDS OF HEAVEN

heavens can also be rendered the four winds of the heavens. Where did we hear that term used before?

THE FOUR WINDS

The four winds are these four horses in the Bible. Zechariah's vision provides us with descriptive characteristics as to their accomplishments when set loose upon the world.

Notice the directions Zechariah was shown that the horses went.

> *The black horses which are therein go forth into the north country; and the white go forth after them; and the grisled go forth toward the south country. And the bay went forth, and sought to go that they might walk to and fro through the earth: and he said, Get you hence, walk to and fro through the earth. So they walked to and fro through the earth. Zechariah 6:6-7*

Black went to the North. The White horses were said to follow these black horses. But something very profound is noted if you read the same verses in the Contemporary English Version and the NIV, for in them we distinctly read the White traveled to the West!

> Zechariah 6:6 CEV *The chariot with black horses goes toward the north, the chariot with white horses goes toward the west, and the one with spotted horses goes toward the south."*

The Grisled horses went south.

137

TAKE A BITE OF ETERNAL LIFE

In Zechariah's vision, instead of a pale horse, we read of the Grisled and Bay. The Grisled went south, while the Bay went throughout the whole world. But the point is that there was a duo of horses in the fourth set. Grisled and Bay. Each of these split and moved in different directions. Notice the fourth horse in Revelation:

> *And I looked, and behold a pale horse: and his name*
> *that sat on him was Death, and Hell followed with him...*
> *Revelation 6:8*

Death was the key thought, and hell followed with him. There we see the dual aspect, just as Zechariah's vision saw two aspects in the fourth set of horses!

WHERE THE HORSES TRAVELED

Zechariah saw the horses travel in directions that seem to correspond to the positioning of the Beasts as represented by the standards of Israel. But this is not noticed upon first glance. There seems to be a contrary direction in which the horses travel in Zechariah's visions, when compared to the compass points with which these horses were associated in their connection with the Beasts or Cherubims of Revelation 6. As we stated, the North standard of the eagle corresponded to the fourth Horse which was Pale. And this pointed to the Grisled and Bay horses. However, in Zechariah's vision, the Grisled horses traveled south, while the corresponding Eagle was north of the Tabernacle. What is the reason for this?

> *...and the grisled go forth toward the south country.*
> *Zechariah 6:6*

THE FOUR WINDS OF HEAVEN

Let us also notice the seeming opposite direction in which the black horses travel when compared to their corresponding Beast, the man. Reuben's standard, the man, stood south.

> *The black horses which are therein go forth into the north country; Zechariah 6:6*

The black travel to the North, but the corresponding Beast stood at the South of the Tabernacle.

Yet there is valid reasoning behind this if we consider the camps about the Tabernacle and the purpose of the positioning of the banners.

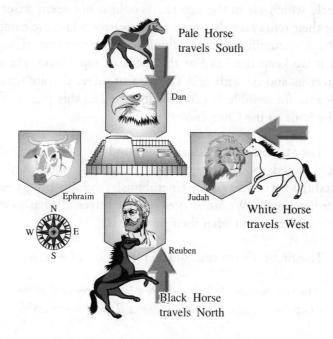

Pale Horse travels South

Dan

Ephraim

Judah

White Horse travels West

N
W   E
S

Reuben

Black Horse travels North

TAKE A BITE OF ETERNAL LIFE

We read about the directions of the white, black and grisled horses in Zechariah 6, but we do not read about the red horses going anywhere. However, we cannot deny there is a definite pattern here that is associated with the placement of the tribal standards and their association with the horses as related in Revelation 6. We only wish to emphasize that a pattern is formed in this picture. This prophecy in Zechariah is not *exact* in its comparison with Revelation 6 and the issue of the Tabernacle standards, but it is most certainly a pattern that is in agreement with all of the rest.

The positions of the four camps about the Tabernacle exposed the backs of the people to potential attackers, since the tent openings faced inwards to the direction of the Tabernacle which sat in the centre. Would it not seem wiser to have their tents face the outer region surrounding the camps? Perhaps, naturally, we might think so. Is it not true, though, that if we keep the Lord as the focus of our vision, He will protect us and be with us? The idea of safety despite natural concerns for trouble is certainly involved in this picture due to the issue of the Cherubims.

The standards positioned all around the camps were definitely linked to the thought of Cherubims, since they depicted the very faces of the Cherubims! And this brings us to a further point. We must now ask ourselves, "What exactly are Cherubims, and what their purpose is?"

The first time we read of Cherubims is in Genesis.

So he drove out the man; and he placed at the east of the Garden of Eden Cherubims, and a flaming sword which

turned every way, to keep the way of the tree of life.
Genesis 3:24

They Cherubims would keep the way of the Garden. They were guardians.

These faces upon the Cherubims, as seen in Ezekiel and Revelation, have a strong connection to Adam before he fell from the Garden life with God, for Adam named certain classes of animals which correlate with these faces.

And Adam gave names to all cattle, and to the fowl of the air, and to every Beast of the field; but for Adam there was not found an help meet for him. Genesis 2:20

In Hebrew culture, the lion is the king of the Beasts, the ox is the king of the cattle and the eagle is the king of the fowl. In other words, Adam named the creatures that are represented by the faces on the Cherubims! He also called his mate "woman" in the next few verses, so we see a picture of Adam's authority over all the creatures in the scene where he names these animals, including humanity.

When Adam fell from the Garden, he lost his authority and became a tiller of the ground. When Adam saw Cherubims facing him at the Garden entrance as a barrier, with the very faces of the creatures he named during the days of his authority, he was reminded of the place of authority from which he fell. It was almost as though the Cherubims were silent witness to the fact that he fell from authority, and said, "To stand beyond this point is to be in authority with God over earth."

TAKE A BITE OF ETERNAL LIFE

Mankind would one day return to that place of authority.

In all of this, so far, we see Cherubims as guardians and emblems of the authority first given to Adam and Eve before the fall.

Consider also that these creatures were depicted upon the veil of the Temple.

> *Moreover thou shalt make the Tabernacle with ten curtains of fine twined linen, and blue, and purple, and scarlet: with Cherubims of cunning work shalt thou make them. Exodus 26:1*

And they were depicted upon the Mercy Seat in a guardian-type fashion, too.

> *And thou shalt make two Cherubims of gold, of beaten work shalt thou make them, in the two ends of the mercy seat. And make one cherub on the one end, and the other cherub on the other end: even of the mercy seat shall ye make the Cherubims on the two ends thereof. And the Cherubims shall stretch forth their wings on high, covering the mercy seat with their wings, and their faces shall look one to another; toward the mercy seat shall the faces of the Cherubims be. Exodus 25:18-20*

So we find they are definitely guardians and reminders of Adam's place of authority. Just as the Cherubims blocked the Garden's entrance, the Cherubims on the veil blocked man from entering the holiest of holies in the Tabernacle and Temple. In other words, the Holiest of Holies represented that place of authority with God from which man fell.

THE FOUR WINDS OF HEAVEN

Regardless, therefore, of any natural worries over potential danger of encamping around the Tabernacle, while their backs were exposed to any enemy, we see a beautiful picture of God's guardianship about us!

THE MOST HOLY PLACE – MODEL OF THE GARDEN OF EDEN

Now, with this in mind, we can see that the picture of the Cherubims on the four banners of the camps of Israel around the Tabernacle in the wilderness (Numbers 2) show God's people who have authority with Him, Who is in their midst. God's presence literally dwelt in *the midst* of the camps inside the Tabernacle.

The standards stood for the four camps of God's people! Many people assume Cherubims to be Angels. This does not seem to be the case at all. The faces of the Cherubims on the standards did not stand in place of Angels, but stood as the people of Israel who were positioned around God's presence!

Let me also point out that these Cherubims, called Beasts in Revelation, are said to have spoken certain words, giving us a clue as to their identity.

And when he had taken the book, the four Beasts and four and twenty elders fell down before the Lamb, having every one of them harps, and golden vials full of odours, which are the prayers of saints. And they sung a new song, saying, Thou art worthy to take the book, and to open the seals thereof: for thou wast slain, and hast redeemed us to God by thy blood out of every kindred, and tongue, and people, and nation; And hast made us unto

143

our God kings and priests: and we shall reign on the earth. Revelation 5:8-10

The Beasts cry, "Thou hast redeemed us to God by the blood out of every kindred, and tongue, and people, and nation." Are Angels redeemed by the blood of Jesus? No. These Cherubims/Beasts are nothing less than representative of the members of the Church of the living God! As the standards around the Tabernacle stood for the tribes of God's people, Israel, these Beasts symbolized God's Church, also! They were redeemed by the blood of Jesus! They are the redeemed from the tribes, nations, people and tongues of the human race!

When the tribes were placed around the Tabernacle, their backs were exposed to the presence of an enemy that might be in the area. With their tents facing inward to the Tabernacle, they portrayed the boldness and faith in God's providence to protect them. They had no fear, for we do not look to our enemy and its great threat, but we look instead to God Who is our strength when trouble comes. And no weapon formed against us shall prosper.

This is also seen in the picture of the Cherubims situated atop the mercy seat. They look inward to the mercy seat where the blood of atonement was sprinkled seven times on the Day of Atonement. Since the blood is the embodiment of all the work of Jesus Christ in His death, burial and resurrection, we see that our eyes of faith must be fixed upon the truths of the Gospel that we might stand strong in the anointing power of God!

THE FOUR WINDS OF HEAVEN

The southern face of Reuben's banner bore the likeness of the third Beast, a man. The corresponding horse in Revelation 6 was the black horse which traveled to the north. We can, therefore, see that there was *a particular grace of God upon His people*. This grace prevents the black horse of famine from attacking them as they were in camp!

If an enemy is traveling northward towards its prey, it would mean the enemy comes upward from the south, from the prey's perspective. This shows us a mighty truth! The picture of these horses, also called winds or spirits, traveled towards the Tabernacle. This shows the enemy's attempts to attack and overcome God's people. It explains why the standards were positioned in compass locations opposite to the directions in which the horses traveled.

We face-off against the enemy, in Jesus' name! No weapon formed against us shall prosper! Whether the enemy's weapon be famine (the spirit of the Black horse), or any other enemy, we can overcome! We have the anointing! And the reason the Third Beast was positioned south in correspondence to the black horse, was to enable it to prevent that northward traveling spirit from coming from their southern direction to hurt God's people. It was the southern defense against a north-bound traveling enemy!

The grisled horses went south towards the camp and were prevented from successfully attacking and overcoming the camp by the positioning of the fourth Beast, the eagle, at the camp's north side. The White horses raced westward, according the NIV and CEV, towards the Tabernacle only to be confronted by the anointing of the Lion at the east of the Tabernacle.

Although the bay horses went in other directions than that which would seem to correspond to this thinking, we can still see a definite pattern for this reasoning. The fact is obviously considered that God might redirect the horses in His wrath to attack those areas not always corresponding to the general trend of direction they may take. There is enough scriptural precedent in Zechariah 6 to indicate this pattern of thought is correct.

Zechariah's vision involved a picture of God's wrath being vented upon the enemies of God in the particular regions the horses traveled.

> *Then cried he upon me, and spake unto me, saying, Behold, these that go toward the north country have quieted my spirit in the north country. Zechariah 6:8*

Aside from the thought of the Tabernacle, in Zechariah's day, the northern country corresponded to Syria and those nations north of Israel. This region of people sinned in such a manner that God's wrath would be quieted, or satisfied, by the judgment of the black horses that traveled their way. The black horses represented the spirit of famine. Famine would strike the northern country where Babylon and Syria dwelt.

The horses that went south were the grisled horses. They represented death. Hell is seen in the Bay horses which went throughout the whole world in God's anger. Therefore, in normal conditions when Israel served God righteously, these forces were prevented from attacking God's people by His power of anointing upon them. God assigned an anointing power to each "cherub" to keep it at bay, and thereby keep His people safe.

ANOINTING

There is more truth involved in the issue of the anointing of God upon His Church. Revelation 11:3-4 shows two witnesses who are called "the two olive trees". The mention of these two witnesses connects us to another vision of Zechariah.

And I will give power unto my two witnesses, and they shall prophesy a thousand two hundred and threescore days, clothed in sackcloth. These are the two olive trees, and the two candlesticks standing before the God of the earth. Revelation 11:3-4

We do not read they were simply two average olive trees, but were specifically, "the" olive trees. In other words, they were a particular two. That can only mean there was a precedent of a certain two olive trees we are supposed to consider in the Bible elsewhere after reading this scripture. Look to the rest of the Bible! There is a note in Zechariah 4 which refers to Zerubbabel and Joshua as two olive trees. These men were rebuilding the Temple in Zechariah's day. They are said to be the two anointed ones immediately after we read of Jerusalem having been measured. Notice that Revelation 11:1-2, where we read of the two olive trees, also included words about John having been told to also measure the Temple.

Then answered I, and said unto him, What are these two olive trees upon the right side of the candlestick and upon the left side thereof? And I answered again, and said unto him, What be these two olive branches which through the two golden pipes empty the golden oil out of

TAKE A BITE OF ETERNAL LIFE

*themselves? And he answered me and said, Knowest thou
not what these be? And I said, No, my lord. Then said
he, These are the two anointed ones, that stand by the
Lord of the whole earth. Zechariah 4:11-14*

And there is a third reference in the bible that ties Cherubims in with the thought of two olive trees.

*And within the oracle he made two Cherubims of olive
tree, each ten cubits high. 1 Kings 6:23*

Two olive trees were fashioned in the shape of two Cherubims in Solomon's Temple. So, in 1 Kings, the two olive
trees were Cherubims. We can then see that the thought of
witness or anointing is also linked to the thought of Cherubims. Anointing oil was derived from the olive. The olive
trees represent God's anointed people who are anointed to
restore that which Adam lost. Since Zechariah saw a vision
of a man measuring the City, and heard one tell this man that
Jerusalem shall be inhabited again (Zechariah 2), we see the
thought of restoration. Israel had just returned from Babylonian captivity at that time in order to re-inhabit the City. Before we read of the two olive trees in Revelation 11, the picture we see is one of John measuring the Temple as well.
Combined together, these visions illustrate the restoration of
the Temple of God, which speaks of His people. The Temple always foreshadowed God's people, the Church.

What is the greatest restoration of all? Whatever it is, it
is the meaning behind Revelation 11. The restoration of man
to pre-fall status with God, as Adam enjoyed it, is paramount
in God's plans. The Cherubims represent the restored authority in the church that man had over the world. Recall

148

that Adam named the very creatures that were represented by the faces of the Cherubims. And these same Cherubims are called two olive trees in Solomon's Temple (another link to the thought of Temple!), signifying anointing. With all of this in mind, we see further confirmation that the Cherubims figured around the Tabernacle on the banners of the camps represent the anointing upon God's people!

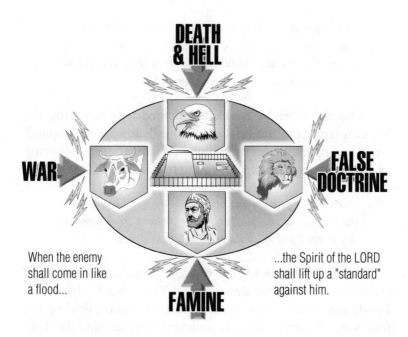

DEATH & HELL

WAR

FALSE DOCTRINE

FAMINE

When the enemy shall come in like a flood...

...the Spirit of the LORD shall lift up a "standard" against him.

13

THE FOUR ANGELS

As we turn back to the book of Revelation, we see even further clarification of the four winds of the heavens, or the four spirits noted in regards to the four horses.

And after these things I saw four angels standing on the four corners of the earth, holding the four winds of the earth, that the wind should not blow on the earth, nor on the sea, nor on any tree. Revelation 7:1

This is written in Revelation immediately following the 6th chapter where the horses and the Beasts are mentioned. Once again, compare the above verse with the following words of the angel in regards to the four horses of Zechariah.

And the angel answered and said unto me, These are the four spirits of the heavens, which go forth from standing before the Lord of all the earth. Zechariah 6:5

Zechariah was told that the four spirits, or four winds, are the four horses of destruction. The seventh chapter of Revelation informs us that there are four angels "holding the four winds." Just as with the standards surrounding the Tabernacle, this withholding force of the four angels represents God's power warding off any weapon formed against God's people – be it an attack of famine, false doctrine or persecution. God's anointing is upon us!

As we look at the faces of the Cherubims that represent the anointing and authority of God upon us, there is indication of four particular kinds of anointing. The Lion of the Cherubims seems to represent the courage and boldness of the child of God who stands by the God of the earth (as the two witnesses stood) in anointing. The Ox represents the faithful servitude to Christ, and the Eagle indicates the faith that soars above the clouds as an eagle. The Human face reveals the thought of compassion and wisdom in His people, just as the Son of Man, Himself, loved people. All these graces are upon those anointed by His Spirit!

MATTHEW 24

Jesus responded to the disciples' comment of the glorious appearance of the Temple as follows:

> *And Jesus said unto them, See ye not all these things?*
> *verily I say unto you, There shall not be left here one stone*
> *upon another, that shall not be thrown down. And as he*
> *sat upon the mount of Olives, the disciples came unto him*
> *privately, saying, Tell us, when shall these things be? and*
> *what shall be the sign of thy coming, and of the end of the*
> *world? Matthew 24:2-3*

If you will compare Revelation 6 with Matthew 24, you will find that the series of seals, with the first four seals consisting of the four horses, perfectly matches the list of events spoken by Jesus. From the White Horse of false Christs, through to the sixth seal of the sun turning black and the moon to blood, all the events of Revelation 6 are listed in precisely the same order in Matthew 24! Therefore, Jesus' words in Matthew 24 give us the interpretation represented by the four horses!

We know about the Horses' purpose and identities by reading of their effects they cause wherever they go. For example, the White Horse goes forth conquering and to conquer. But what actually is the White Horse? In comparing Matthew 24 with Revelation 6, we find Jesus revealed it is false religion and false Christianity. Notice the first element Jesus warned as being a sign of the end when all the stones of the Temple shall be overturned. This first element corresponds perfectly with the first horseman. And the following four elements He notes correspond, also, with the four horses in Revelation 6 perfectly.

WHITE HORSE-FALSE RELIGION

And Jesus answered and said unto them, Take heed that no man deceive you. For many shall come in my name, saying, I am Christ; and shall deceive many. And ye shall hear of wars and rumours of wars: see that ye be not troubled: for all these things must come to pass, but the end is not yet. Matthew 24:4-6

And I saw, and behold a white horse: and he that sat on him had a bow; and a crown was given unto him: and he went forth conquering, and to conquer. Revelation 6:2

Perhaps the reference to the Lion corresponding to the White Horse depicts the True Christ, the Lion of Judah, as the truth as opposed to False Christs.

RED HORSE-WARS

For nation shall rise against nation, and kingdom against kingdom: ... Matthew 24:7

And there went out another horse that was red: and power was given to him that sat thereon to take peace from the earth, and that they should kill one another: and there was given unto him a great sword. Revelation 6:4

BLACK HORSE-FAMINE

...and there shall be famines, and pestilences, and earthquakes, in divers places. All these are the beginning of sorrows. Matthew 24:7-8

And when he had opened the third seal, I heard the third Beast say, Come and see. And I beheld, and lo a black horse; and he that sat on him had a pair of balances in his hand. And I heard a voice in the midst of the four Beasts say, A measure of wheat for a penny, and three measures of barley for a penny; and see thou hurt not the oil and the wine. Revelation 6:5-6

PALE HORSE-DEATH

Then shall they deliver you up to be afflicted, and shall kill you: and ye shall be hated of all nations for my name's sake. Matthew 24:9

And I looked, and behold a pale horse: and his name that sat on him was Death, and Hell followed with him. And power was given unto them over the fourth part of

153

the earth, to kill with sword, and with hunger, and with death, and with the Beasts of the earth. Revelation 6:8

These horses or spirits will attempt to attack God's elect. Yet God will deliver us out of them all, as follows:

Immediately after the tribulation of those days shall the sun be darkened, and the moon shall not give her light, and the stars shall fall from heaven, and the powers of the heavens shall be shaken: And then shall appear the sign of the Son of man in heaven: and then shall all the tribes of the earth mourn, and they shall see the Son of man coming in the clouds of heaven with power and great glory. And he shall send his angels with a great sound of a trumpet, and they shall gather together his elect from the four winds, from one end of heaven to the other. Matthew 24:29-31

"...from the four winds." These four winds are the Four Horsemen! They are the four spirits of the heavens, as Zechariah discovered.

Let us recall Zechariah's vision and the following truths revealed to him, and compare them, once again, with Matthew 24:31

In the first chariot were red horses; and in the second chariot black horses; And in the third chariot white horses; and in the fourth chariot grisled and bay horses. Then I answered and said unto the angel that talked with me, What are these, my lord? And the angel answered and said unto me, These are the four spirits (Hebrew:

154

*"four winds") of the heavens, which go forth from standing
before the Lord of all the earth. Zechariah 6:2-5*

God shall send His anointing upon His people to deliver
us from the four winds of demonic attack.

REVELATION CHAPTERS 6 AND 7

We have seen all four horses of the first four seals of
Revelation 6 listed in identical order in Matthew 24. But that
is not all that is identical. What about the next few seals?
Sure enough, the entire picture of Revelation 6 and 7 is explained by Jesus Christ in Matthew 24.

The fourth horse that was pale, spoke of death and the
grave. That was the fourth seal. Notably, the fifth seal
speaks of the martyrs of the Lord. This event follows quite
fittingly after the entities of both death and the grave have
gone forth to slay in the fourth seal. What do you have after
a slaying? You have martyrs. Jesus commented, "They shall
deliver up to be afflicted and shall kill you."

We are also given a note to endure and wait after Christ
mentioned the slaying of martyrs in Matthew 24.

*But he that shall endure unto the end, the same shall be
saved. Matthew 24:13*

And there is a note of waiting in Revelation's 5th seal.

*And when he had opened the fifth seal, I saw under the
altar the souls of them that were slain for the word of
God, and for the testimony which they held: And they*

155

cried with a loud voice, saying, How long, O Lord, holy and true, dost thou not judge and avenge our blood on them that dwell on the earth? And white robes were given unto every one of them; and it was said unto them, that they should rest yet for a little season, until their fellowservants also and their brethren, that should be killed as they were, should be fulfilled. Revelation 6:9-11

After the note about martyrdom, Jesus made comments about false Christs once again, and how we should not seek after them. He eventually mentioned the issue of a time when the sun turns black and the moon turns to blood. This is what the sixth seal spoke about.

Immediately after the tribulation of those days shall the sun be darkened, and the moon shall not give her light, and the stars shall fall from heaven, and the powers of the heavens shall be shaken: Matthew 24:29

And I beheld when he had opened the sixth seal, and, lo, there was a great earthquake; and the sun became black as sackcloth of hair, and the moon became as blood; And the stars of heaven fell unto the earth, even as a fig tree casteth her untimely figs, when she is shaken of a mighty wind. And the heaven departed as a scroll when it is rolled together; and every mountain and island were moved out of their places. Revelation 6:12-14

Following the pattern of comparison with Matthew 24, Revelation even went so far as saying that the stars fell from heaven as a fig tree casts her untimely figs. And that is precisely the illustration Jesus used, also.

THE FOUR ANGELS

Now learn a parable of the fig tree; When his branch is yet tender, and putteth forth leaves, ye know that summer is nigh: So likewise ye, when ye shall see all these things, know that it is near, even at the doors.
Matthew 24:32-33

Now that we know there is a definite correlation between the words of Christ in Matthew and Revelation 6's vision of John, we can clarify each seal's identity by adding the thoughts of Jesus to them. Upon comparison, we can discover that the elements of the four horsemen were tribulation elements. This is based upon the realization that Jesus' corresponding statements about them regard them as tribulation elements. In other words, God's people will experience them. Jesus told the disciples they would personally experience these things. Look at the personal pronouns, "you" and "ye" throughout verses 4 through 12. They are associated with tribulation because of a statement Jesus made after having discussed all of the previous events:

Immediately after the tribulation of those days ...
Matthew 24:29

From the first seal to the fifth seal, we find that the events listed were tribulation events. How many times did the Lord and the Apostles speak about the tribulations we will face as Christians?

After the sixth seal is opened we read:

And the kings of the earth, and the great men, and the rich men, and the chief captains, and the mighty men, and every bondman, and every free man, hid themselves in the

157

dens and in the rocks of the mountains; And said to the
mountains and rocks, Fall on us, and hide us from the
face of him that sitteth on the throne, and from the wrath
of the Lamb: For the great day of His wrath is come;
and who shall be able to stand? Revelation 6:15-17

So, Matthew 24:5-28 regard the tribulation aspects of the
Church experiencing the onslaught four horses but being delivered from them when God's wrath is ready to be poured
out upon the earth. God's wrath upon His enemies follows
the tribulation experiences.

Like Lightning

We have found very overwhelming connections between
Zechariah's vision of the horses, Ezekiel's visions of the Cherubims and John's visions of the Beasts. Is it any wonder that
a little note Ezekiel mentioned in regards to his vision of the
Cherubims is also included in Jesus words?

And the living creatures ran and returned as the
appearance of a flash of lightning. Ezekiel 1:14

Connect this with:

For as the lightning cometh out of the east, and shineth
even unto the west; so shall also the coming of the Son of
man be. Matthew 24:27

It seems that Christ rides in the chariot Ezekiel saw with
the four angels whom He shall send to gather His elect from
the four winds. And Ezekiel's chariot does indeed indicate
that Christ sits on a throne on this chariot.

158

THE FOUR ANGELS

And above the firmament that was over their heads was the likeness of a throne, as the appearance of a sapphire stone: and upon the likeness of the throne was the likeness as the appearance of a man above upon it. And I saw as the colour of amber, as the appearance of fire round about within it, from the appearance of his loins even upward, and from the appearance of his loins even downward, I saw as it were the appearance of fire, and it had brightness round about. As the appearance of the bow that is in the cloud in the day of rain, so was the appearance of the brightness round about. This was the appearance of the likeness of the glory of the LORD. And when I saw it, I fell upon my face, and I heard a voice of one that spake. Ezekiel 1:26-28

God's people are in tribulation. I believe this principle applies to any time of tribulation no matter what time of history we may be concerned with. For sure, this points specifically to a certain point in time, but my book is not written with that in mind. God works in certain ways. He always tends to come in power and glory when His people are in trouble. He may not come when we would like to see Him come, but He always comes at just the right time in His eternal schedule.

And he shall send his angels with a great sound of a trumpet, and they shall gather together his elect from the four winds, from one end of heaven to the other. Matthew 24:31

The chariot of Ezekiel represents the anointed Church of God with power to resist attacks of evil. He is in the midst of two or three who are gathered in His name in unity of the

Spirit. That is what Ezekiel saw in the throne amidst the four Cherubims.

Seeing that the two elements of death and grave in the fourth horseman of Revelation 6 leave martyrs, as noted in the next, fifth seal, we can appreciate how God can deliver the church from the four winds by the anointing and power of His Spirit.

You might note that many believers have died and were not delivered from their deaths. That is correct. However, do not forget that the greatest deliverance is leaving this world while holding the victory, not having bowed down to the threats of the devil. Many are the martyrs who have given their lives for the Gospel's sake. However, others are intended to be delivered from death, for their time of death has not yet arrived. Whatever the case, rest assured that God's will is to be accomplished, whether we live or whether we die.

SEALING THE 144,000

Revelation 7 reads of 12,000 Israelites from each of twelve tribes.

And I heard the number of them which were sealed: and there were sealed an hundred and forty and four thousand of all the tribes of the children of Israel. Revelation 7:4

Let me quickly note that the 144,000 do not seem to be literal Israelites of the nation of Israel, as many might suppose. Yes, it does say there are 12,000 from each tribe of Israel. But look more closely. We read that there were 12,000 people sealed from all the tribes of Israel.

THE FOUR ANGELS

The tribes listed in Revelation 7 are:

Judah
Reuben
Gad
Aser
Nephthalim
Manasses
Simeon
Levi
Issachar
Zabulon
Joseph
Benjamin

The order of their births listed in the Genesis chapters 29 and 30 was Reuben, Simeon, Levi, Judah, Dan, Naphtali, Gad, Asher, Issachar, Zebulun, Joseph, Benjamin.

When Jacob blessed his sons, the order is changed somewhat: Reuben, Simeon, Levi, Judah, Zebulun, Issachar, Dan, Gad, Asher, Naphtali, Joseph, Benjamin.

Moses blessed the tribes as well in even a different order again: Reuben, Judah, Levi, Benjamin, Joseph, Zebulun, Issachar, Gad, Dan, Naphtali, Asher. Simeon was not even mentioned.

In Ezekiel 48:31-34, we read of city gates with the names of the tribes listed as follows: Reuben, Judah, Levi, Joseph, Benjamin, Dan, Simeon, Issachar, Zebulun, Gad, Asher and Naphtali.

161

TAKE A BITE OF ETERNAL LIFE

This differs from the list in the Ezekiel 48:1-27: Dan, Asher, Naphtali, Manasseh, Ephraim, Reuben, Judah, Benjamin, Simeon, Issachar, Zebulun, Gad.

In 1 Chronicles chapters 4 through 8, Zebulun and Dan are missing.

The differences were made in consideration of their order of birth, or their geographical positions. Judah was never mentioned first in any other part of the Bible's lists of the tribes. What is also interesting in Revelation 7 is that both Joseph and Manasseh are named, when Joseph never actually was a tribe. Numbers 13:11 indicates that reference to Joseph would actually be reference to the tribe of Manasseh. It is therefore extremely odd to mention both Joseph and Manasseh as two distinct tribes in this list in Revelation 7.

Now, it is interesting to note that the Tribe of Dan is missing from this list. Some say it is due to Judges 18:30's note about Dan's people having committed idolatry. However, this is not referring to natural Israel. It is God's people, the Church, who are the "Israel of God" spiritually speaking (Galatians 6:16).

Notice the number: 144,000. The New Jerusalem, the City of God, is measured as 12,000 furlongs wide, 12,000 furlongs high and 12,000 furlongs in depth. It is a cube. There are 12 edges, not sides, in a cube. That would add up to 12 X 12,000 furlongs, equaling 144,000 furlongs of support edges to the city. And it is no coincidence that there are 144,000 sealed believers.

162

THE FOUR ANGELS

This New City is not a literal set of buildings. John heard the proclamation that the City was the Bride adorned for her husband. Is Jesus marrying a set of buildings? I think not! He is espoused to the Church, His Bride! And Jesus also said, "Ye are the light of the world, a city that is set on a hill cannot be hid." We are the City!

With that in mind, after the Sixth Seal is opened, we come to the chapter of Revelation that speaks of the sealing of the 144,000. We read of the four angels holding back the four winds for the sealing of the 144,000.

> *And I saw another angel ascending from the east, having the seal of the living God: and he cried with a loud voice to the four angels, to whom it was given to hurt the earth and the sea, Saying, Hurt not the earth, neither the sea, nor the trees, till we have sealed the servants of our God in their foreheads. And I heard the number of them which were sealed: and there were sealed an hundred and forty and four thousand of all the tribes of the children of Israel. Revelation 7:2-4*

Praise God, once again we see protection from the four winds, or the four horses! God's anointing keeps us safe. It protects us. If God wants you continue to live in this world and do His will in this earth, you can rest assured that you will be delivered out of the midst of any trouble, whenever you encounter an assault of the four horses and experience tribulation.

After referring to the four horses in verses 4 to 9, Jesus said the following:

TAKE A BITE OF ETERNAL LIFE

But he that shall endure unto the end, the same shall be saved. Matthew 24:13

This statement points ahead to Matthew 24:31's note of gathering the elect from the four winds. After the tribulation of those days, God's people who endure are indeed delivered. They are saved! When God sees us endure tribulation (now or in the future), He will deliver those who stood the test after the time of testing is over. They are saved from it – or gathered from it. They are delivered!

As the Cherubims keep watch and spread their wings over the mercy seat, all we who are seated with Christ in heavenly places are kept in safety by God's anointing.

Could it be that some of God's people are protected while others are not during times of trouble?

Because thou hast kept the word of my patience, I also will keep thee from the hour of temptation, which shall come upon all of the world, to try them that dwell upon the earth. Revelation 3:10

Watch ye therefore, and pray always, that ye may be accounted worthy to escape all these things that shall come to pass, and to stand before the Son of man. Luke 21:36

To escape speaks of being in the midst of trouble, but yet kept, or protected, from its damage.

14

AT HIS RIGHT HAND...

*And I saw in the right hand of him that sat on the throne
a book written within and on the backside, sealed with
seven seals. And I saw a strong angel proclaiming with a
loud voice, Who is worthy to open the book, and to loose
the seals thereof? And no man in heaven, nor in earth,
neither under the earth, was able to open the book, neither
to look thereon. And I wept much, because no man was
found worthy to open and to read the book, neither to look
thereon. And one of the elders saith unto me, Weep not:
behold, the Lion of the tribe of Juda, the Root of David,
hath prevailed to open the book, and to loose the seven
seals thereof. Revelation 5:1-5*

The salvation of mankind is involved in this pattern.
We see a pattern found in the work of Calvary
through which God chose to save souls.

*And I beheld, and, lo, in the midst of the throne and of
the four Beasts, and in the midst of the elders, stood a
Lamb as it had been slain, having seven horns and seven
eyes, which are the seven Spirits of God sent forth into all
the earth. Revelation 5:6*

How could a lamb stand after it had been slain?

And they sung a new song, saying, Thou art worthy to take the book, and to open the seals thereof: for thou wast slain, and hast redeemed us to God by thy blood out of every kindred, and tongue, and people, and nation; Revelation 5:9

He redeemed us when He took the book, after entering the Holiest of Holies with His own blood.

REVELATION AFFECTS OUR HEARTS

In Matthew 13:10-17, Jesus spoke of people whose hearts are waxed gross so that they cannot see nor hear. In that text, Jesus said that a person is blessed if they can see and hear, or understand.

When Jesus asked the disciples whom they thought He was, Peter said he was the Christ, the Son of the living God. Jesus remarked and said that Peter was blessed, because flesh and blood did not reveal that to Him, but rather God the Father revealed it. To be blessed is to enjoy the bliss of Heaven. Since only God can show us hidden truths that flesh and blood cannot relate to us, we are certainly blessed of God to be made privy to such mysteries.

If all that we know is what other people have related to us, then we have not received revelation. This sort of revelation can only come from God. Even people who received it themselves cannot give it to you, because flesh and blood does not reveal such things to others. In order to be blessed, you must experience the reception of revelation from God, Himself. Something actually opens up to your heart as God directly intervenes there in your life.

166

Most Pharisees, who could neither make heads nor tails out of Jesus' parables, were intellectually superior to the disciples of Jesus. And if flesh and blood could reveal such things to people, these Pharisees surely would have received them before anyone else. But these intellectuals missed out on many of the things Jesus taught. His parables were in just such a form that one had to receive help from God in order to get their full meanings. One had to be blessed in order to enjoy such revelations. God had to be involved.

It's not our intellects that can relate to these things. It's our hearts. These Pharisees' hearts had waxed gross. Paul spoke about this same dilemma.

> But their minds were blinded: for until this day remaineth the same vail untaken away in the reading of the old testament; which vail is done away in Christ. But even unto this day, when Moses is read, the vail is upon their heart. Nevertheless when it shall turn to the Lord, the vail shall be taken away. 2 Corinthians 3:14-16

REPENT AND BE UNVEILED

A veil is situated over the heart, and that is what Jesus meant when He said their "hearts are waxed gross." It's not more education that will do the trick, but a turning of the heart.

Consider the thought of the term "repent," often used by Jesus and the Apostles. The definition of "repent" is "to turn around." Turning your heart around towards Jesus is a genuine change of everything you are. It's not making believe you are a Christian, while continuing to sin behind everyone's back. I cannot read your mind nor see what is in your heart, but God can. He simply will not give revelation to one whose heart is not truly turned or repentant. We must be sincere.

Moses *turned* aside to see the burning bush and God spoke to him. John heard a voice like a trumpet behind him, in Revelation 1:10-12 and *turned* towards it.

Furthermore, a voice like a trumpet is indicative of revelation being given.

> *Cry aloud, spare not, lift up thy voice like a trumpet, and shew my people ... Isaiah 58:1*

Revelation is the divine revealing of truth to a person, and Isaiah said that showing God's people truth is accomplished by lifting up one's voice like a trumpet.

John also heard a voice like a trumpet later on in Revelation's account of his visions:

> *After this I looked, and, behold, a door was opened in heaven: and the first voice which I heard was as it were of a trumpet talking with me; which said, Come up hither, and I will shew thee things which must be hereafter. Revelation 4:1*

"A voice like a trumpet." And in both cases, the prophet was shown truths. "I will shew thee..." This is the giving of revelation. A door is opened and John peered into Heaven.

Flesh and blood did not reveal these things to John. Jesus revealed them by His Spirit.

Isn't it interesting that Jesus told Peter that the Father reveals (*revelates*) things to us, and we read where the voice like a trumpet, God's revelation, came from a surprising source...

> *And I turned to see the voice that spake with me. And being turned, I saw seven golden candlesticks; And in the midst of the seven candlesticks one like unto the Son of man, clothed with a garment down to the foot, and girt about the paps with a golden girdle. Revelation 1:12-13*

Always remember that the head is the part of our bodies that thinks, whereas the heart believes. Now, the natural part of humanity is the part that both sinners and saints alike make use of. And that includes intellect.

> *Now we have received, not the spirit of the world, but the spirit which is of God; that we might know the things that are freely given to us of God. Which things also we speak, not in the words which man's wisdom teacheth, but which the Holy Ghost teacheth; comparing spiritual things with spiritual. But the natural man receiveth not the things of the Spirit of God: for they are foolishness unto him: neither can he know them, because they are spiritually discerned. 1 Corinthians 2:12-14*

Paul said the natural man cannot receive the things of God. Like the Pharisees' reactions to Jesus' words, the spiritual things sound foolish to the natural man. Our hearts, on the other hand, are involved in this matter.

TAKE A BITE OF ETERNAL LIFE

Paul preached truths that were hidden from mankind since the time of the beginning of the world.

But we speak the wisdom of God in a mystery, even the hidden wisdom, which God ordained before the world unto our glory: 1 Corinthians 2:7

He called it wisdom that was hidden.

Whereby, when ye read, ye may understand my knowledge in the mystery of Christ) Which in other ages was not made known unto the sons of men, as it is now revealed unto his holy apostles and prophets by the Spirit; That the Gentiles should be fellowheirs, and of the same body, and partakers of his promise in Christ by the gospel: Whereof I was made a minister, according to the gift of the grace of God given unto me by the effectual working of his power. Unto me, who am less than the least of all saints, is this grace given, that I should preach among the Gentiles the unsearchable riches of Christ; And to make all men see what is the fellowship of the mystery, which from the beginning of the world hath been hid in God, who created all things by Jesus Christ: Ephesians 3:4-9

Even the mystery which hath been hid from ages and from generations, but now is made manifest to his saints: To whom God would make known what is the riches of the glory of this mystery among the Gentiles; which is Christ in you, the hope of glory: Colossians 1:26-27

Look at how many times Paul referred to the Mystery of the Gospel!

The Bible refers to the Gospel as a mystery that was hidden from the beginning of the world. This means that God had the Gospel in mind since before Adam's time. That is the reason Revelation 13:8 says the lamb was slain from the foundation of the world.

SEALED WISDOM

God spoke of visions and things of the Spirit that were hidden from man as sealed books, in the writings of Isaiah.

And the vision of all is become unto you as the words of a book that is sealed, which men deliver to one that is learned, saying, Read this, I pray thee: and he saith, I cannot; for it is sealed: Isaiah 29:11

To the one who is learned in religious issues, a vision may be given and yet never be understood. The learned are the educated and the intellectual. And yet the educated and the intellectual could not understand it. This describes the Pharisees and Scribes quite adequately.

We read in Revelation 5:1 that God holds in His right hand a book that is sealed seven times. The numeral seven signifies "complete" or "perfect" in the Bible, since God completed His work and rested on the seventh day. This symbolizes that the Book in question is perfectly sealed.

And I saw in the right hand of him that sat on the throne a book written within and on the backside, sealed with seven seals. Revelation 5:1

Nobody could open this book. It was perfectly sealed. In other words, nobody could understand the mystery.

Then John heard news that the Lion of Judah was able to open it. John saw a Lamb appear and approach the throne to take the book from the hand of the One sitting on the throne. The lamb was able to take the book when nobody else could take it.

And verse 9 reads:

> ...*Thou art worthy to take the book, and to open the seals thereof: for thou wast slain, and hast redeemed us to God by thy blood out of every kindred, and tongue, and people, and nation; Revelation 5:9*

Everything fits together! The mystery is the Gospel message of Christ in you. And it is opened, or revealed, when the slain lamb stood and then took it. The lamb resurrected! In order for a slain lamb to be found standing, there must have been a resurrection of the lamb.

ONE WITH SEVEN EYES CAN OPEN SEVEN SEALS

> ...*stood a Lamb as it had been slain, having seven horns and seven eyes, which are the seven Spirits of God sent forth into all the earth. Revelation 5:6*

He has seven eyes, because no mystery is hidden from Him. He can see all. He has perfect insight. Hebrews 4:13 informs us that that all things are naked and opened to the eyes of Christ, our High Priest.

AT HIS RIGHT HAND

This lamb is seen with seven horns because He said "All power is given unto me," after He arose from the grave, in Matthew 28:18. Horns represent power in the Bible (Daniel 8:6-7; Habakkuk 3:4; Revelation 17:12).

Many wise men have desired to see these things and have not seen them because they were so perfectly sealed. Only Jesus Christ could unseal them or understand them. Christ had not yet come, and had not yet died and resurrected in the days of the prophets in the Old Testament.

Since Christ has come, preachers like Paul have eyes *of understanding* to see, for they receive revelation from God because their hearts were turned towards Jesus.

VEILS ON HEARTS

You can't fool Jesus! If your heart is living in pretence, God sees it and He will not give you any revelation. Revelation literally means unveiling. Where is the veil that must be removed? It is on the hearts of men and women.

Paul said the mystery was "Christ in you the.... hope of glory." In the letter to the Ephesians, he told us that our eyes must be enlightened to know the hope. In other words, our eyes of understanding must be opened in order that we might receive the revelation.

That the God of our Lord Jesus Christ, the Father of glory, may give unto you the spirit of wisdom and revelation in the knowledge of him: Ephesians 1:17

173

And I saw when the Lamb opened one of the seals, and I
heard, as it were the noise of thunder, one of the four
Beasts saying, Come and see.   And I saw, ...
Revelation 6:1-2a

And John saw!

Oh, God had so much in store for us! But we lost access
to the path of life.   However, those Cherubims barring
Adam's entrance into the Garden represented the Church,
and they stood in the Garden entrance as a message to us.
With eyes all over their bodies, and possessing *all understand-*
ing, the Church is in this world for you to urge you to come
and see.

JESUS IS THE WAY

Is the way into the Garden opened now? Oh, yes!

Jesus said "I AM THE WAY." His death on the cross is
the key that opened that doorway.

In his sermon to the people gathered in Jerusalem on the
day of Pentecost, Peter quoted Psalm 16:10 and referred to
Jesus.

> For *thou wilt not leave my soul in hell; neither wilt thou*
> *suffer thine Holy One to see corruption. Psalm 16:10*

And speaking of the resurrection of Jesus, which is part
of the Gospel, David continued to say...

AT HIS RIGHT HAND

Thou wilt shew me the path of life: in thy presence is fulness of joy; at thy right hand there are pleasures for evermore. Psalm 16:11

In the right hand of God, in Revelation 5, was a book of mystery sealed from the beginning of the world! And Christ's death and resurrection caused it to be opened. John saw all this because He first turned to see Jesus, as recorded in Revelation 1.

What was in the book for 4,000 years before Christ came and unsealed it? What blessing and privileges did it contain? What was there in God's right hand?

" ...at thy right hand there are pleasures for evermore."

We left God's presence, and left joy before we were born, and were yet in Adam's loins when he was cast from the Garden. But through Christ we who are saved have come back again! And in thy presence is fullness of joy. At His right hand there are pleasures for evermore.

Pleasures for how long? Evermore! This speaks of nothing less than eternal life!

Notice the pattern:

First John *turned*.

A person must turn the heart around and truly repent away from one's former lifestyle. Your intellect can pretend to be Christian, but God knows the heart. Unless the heart is turned toward Him, He gives you no revelation. Be sincere. Be real. Truly repent and turn to Him.

Can you see this hope?

There are pleasures forevermore. Fullness of joy!

When God gives us revelation, we are blessed. We experience the bliss of Heaven.

15

JEREMIAH'S SEALED EVIDENCE

In the book of the prophet Jeremiah, we read a very unusual story. Chapter 32 relates the story of the time God told Jeremiah to obey a very strange command. He told him to purchase a piece of property from his cousin, Hanameel, while the Babylonians were marching into Israel, conquering and taking over the nation and enslaving the people.

Why, in anybody's right mind, would they buy land just before an enemy takes it over, and while the enemy cares less about who owned it or who recently sold it or purchased it? What value would it be to buy land that was soon going to be owned on demand by an enemy? What kind of cousin would seek to sell you such land, to begin with?

God, nevertheless, told Jeremiah to go ahead and accept the strange offer from his cousin. So, while the enemy marched towards the city, Jeremiah legally purchased it and signed a deed for the property and sealed it, handing it over to a man named Baruch, a faithful attendant of Jeremiah. Just before the tragedy occurred and Israel was taken captive by the enemy, all of this took place.

Jeremiah sealed a copy of the deed, handed it to Baruch and told him to keep it in a safe place, since it would be a very long time before it would be retrieved again. But it would be retrieved one day. The Lord informed Jeremiah that lands in that region that were presently being taken over by the Babylonians, but would one day be sold and bought once again.

Then Jeremiah prayed to God about all of this, knowing that deliverance would come, but yet feeling it seemed so impossible. Jeremiah related the conditions of the then-present distress to God.

> *Behold the mounts, they are come unto the city to take it; and the city is given into the hand of the Chaldeans, that fight against it, because of the sword, and of the famine, and of the pestilence: and what thou hast spoken is come to pass; and, behold, thou seest it. And thou hast said unto me, O Lord GOD, Buy thee the field for money, and take witnesses; for the city is given into the hand of the Chaldeans. Jeremiah 32:24-25*

He said, "Look, God! See the mounts and the engines of shot! The enemy is right here! And you just told me to buy land that is being approached by the enemy. What gives? You told me to buy this land in a time when it is worth nothing. Is this not a complete waste of my time and money? What are you doing this for?"

> *Then came the word of the LORD unto Jeremiah, saying, Behold, I am the LORD, the God of all flesh: is there any thing too hard for me? Therefore thus saith the LORD; Behold, I will give this city into the hand of the Chaldeans, and into the hand of Nebuchadrezzar king of Babylon, and he shall take it: And the Chaldeans, that*

178

fight against this city, shall come and set fire on this city, and burn it with the houses, upon whose roofs they have offered incense unto Baal, and poured out drink unto other gods, to provoke me to anger. For the children of Israel and the children of Judah have only done evil before me from their youth: for the children of Israel have only provoked me to anger with the work of their hands, saith the LORD. For this city hath been to me as a provocation of mine anger and of my fury from the day that they built it even unto this day; that I should remove it from before my face, Jeremiah 32:26-31

God told him, "Buy the land, Jeremiah. The enemy is coming because Israel disobeyed me. But..."

And now therefore thus saith the LORD, the God of Israel, concerning this city, whereof ye say, It shall be delivered into the hand of the king of Babylon by the sword, and by the famine, and by the pestilence; Behold, I will gather them out of all countries, whither I have driven them in mine anger, and in my fury, and in great wrath; and I will bring them again unto this place, and I will cause them to dwell safely: And they shall be my people, and I will be their God: And I will give them one heart, and one way, that they may fear me for ever, for the good of them, and of their children after them: And I will make an everlasting covenant with them, that I will not turn away from them, to do them good; but I will put my fear in their hearts, that they shall not depart from me. Jeremiah 32:36-40

In other words, "The enemy is coming because man disobeyed me, but I will bring you back again. I will gather you

179

from all nations where I have driven. Rest assured, and you can count your life on it – Israel will return. I commanded you to write a deed and buy the land before the time that the enemy arrived; because it is that sure that I will redeem you one day! The enemy will be dealt with and gone in that day. Israel will be here again. The land may not be worth much when the enemy gets hold of it, and who knows what they will do in the land. But before they take it, I have made up my mind to have it sealed in a deed, to one day hold it again."

ANOTHER SEALED DEED & USELESS PROPERTY

When we read about a book sealed with seven seals in the right hand of God in Revelation 5:1 – about a book that is retrieved by Jesus, the Lamb – we see a parallel with this story! In fact, God used the well-known symbol of Jeremiah and the sealed title deed of property in the vision He gave to John about salvation of mankind. John and those early Christians were very familiar with all the Old Testament stories, including this story of Jeremiah. Being a Jew and raised up under the Old Covenant, John's mind would immediately go to that story upon seeing this vision.

Today, we may not be as familiar with such stories as was John. So please understand that when you read of visions in the Book of Revelation you have to look elsewhere in the Bible to understand what the symbols really speak about. Look in the Bible for the same symbols used in Revelation, and interpret the book properly.

Property had been deeded out, to be redeemed after a long time of the enemy holding the property.

JEREMIAH'S SEALED EVIDENCE

Let us apply this to the overall history of mankind from the beginning of time. Before the enemy ever marched in and seized hold of power in the earth, by having tempted mankind in the Garden of Eden, God saw what would happen. Our Lord looked across time, as only He has the ability to do, and saw Adam disobeying Him before it ever happened. Due to that disobedience, God knew He would cast mankind from the Garden. This same picture was repeated in Jeremiah's day as He drove Israel out into the world into all nations due to their disobedience.

Compare these words:

> *So he drove out the man; and he placed at the east of the Garden of Eden Cherubims, and a flaming sword which turned every way, to keep the way of the tree of life. Genesis 3:24*

> *Behold, I will gather them out of all countries, whither I have driven them in mine anger, and in my fury, and in great wrath; and I will bring them again unto this place, and I will cause them to dwell safely: Jeremiah 32:37*

He drove man out of the Garden as He drove Israel out of their land.

But after Israel was driven out and into the hand of the enemy, God promised to gather them from where He drove them. He would bring them back to the Garden again – back to Himself. And they would dwell safely. In order to do that, though, the enemy of man's soul had to be dealt with.

TAKE A BITE OF ETERNAL LIFE

Now is the judgment of this world: now shall the prince
of this world be cast out. And I, if I be lifted up from the
earth, will draw all men unto me. This he said, signifying
what death he should die. John 12:31-33

Jesus did not refer to our need to worship Him when He
said He must be lifted up. He referred to the sort of death
He should die. When He was about to die, He announced
that then would the enemy be cast out. At that point, He
would draw, or re-gather all men to Himself. This is a perfect
parallel to Jeremiah 32!

Don't look back to the life you lived before you ever
knew God and recall how disgusting you lived and what past
events marred you. Before the enemy took hold of you, due
to Adam's disobedience, God wrote up a deed. Before the
foundation of the world was the Lamb was slain, for at the
foundation of the world, in the beginning times of earth,
mankind disobeyed God and sinned. And the enemy came in
and took over humanity.

While the enemy had you, and you were worthless and
sinful and filthy, going your own way and not His way, blas-
pheming and cursing, God looked past all of that. He waited
for the right time when He would come down into this world
as a man.

According as he hath chosen us in him before the
foundation of the world, that we should be holy and
without blame before him in love: Ephesians 1:4

In hope of eternal life, which God, that cannot lie,
promised before the world began; Titus 1:2

182

JEREMIAH'S SEALED EVIDENCE

Forasmuch as ye know that ye were not redeemed with corruptible things, as silver and gold, from your vain conversation received by tradition from your fathers; But with the precious blood of Christ, as of a lamb without blemish and without spot: Who verily was foreordained before the foundation of the world, but was manifest in these last times for you, Who by him do believe in God, that raised him up from the dead, and gave him glory; that your faith and hope might be in God. Seeing ye have purified your souls in obeying the truth through the Spirit unto unfeigned love of the brethren, see that ye love one another with a pure heart fervently: 1 Peter 1:18-22

...the book of life of the Lamb slain from the foundation of the world. Revelation 13:8

This very book/deed was taken and unsealed after Jesus resurrected from the dead. Two thousand years ago, Jesus said, "Now shall the prince of this world be cast out. If I be lifted up, I will draw all men to me."

And they sung a new song, saying, Thou art worthy to take the book, and to open the seals thereof: for thou wast slain, and hast redeemed us to God by thy blood out of every kindred, and tongue, and people, and nation; Revelation 5:9

We were the property! The title deed included us in the place where we should have been. Time came to drive the enemy out by the cross of Jesus Christ! Time came to destroy the works of the devil. Time came to make mankind worth something again! — time came to clean mankind from all sin and filthiness – to wash away our sins and bring us

183

from every nation back to Himself again. The book of redeemed property – the title deed of what was lost and held by
the enemy – was finally retrieved again!

> *Behold, I will gather them out of all countries, whither I*
> *have driven them in mine anger, and in my fury, and in*
> *great wrath; and I will bring them again unto this place,*
> *and I will cause them to dwell safely: Jeremiah 32:37*

After Jesus took the book in Revelation 5, He opened six
of the seals, having told the disciples He would draw all men
to Himself. That is the reason we read the following words:

> *After this I beheld, and, lo, a great multitude, which no*
> *man could number, of all nations, and kindreds, and*
> *people, and tongues, stood before the throne, and before the*
> *Lamb, clothed with white robes, and palms in their*
> *hands; And cried with a loud voice, saying, Salvation to*
> *our God which sitteth upon the throne, and unto the*
> *Lamb. Revelation 7:9-10*

He did the very thing that was foreshadowed in Jeremiah
32! He gathered to Himself all who were driven into all nations. Jesus said "If I be lifted up, I will draw all men unto
me."

Oh, how the cries went up in praise to God when the
Lamb retrieved the book!

Are you damaged by the past? Did you have a hard time
while the enemy owned you? Don't look down on yourself.
God looks at it as though He's recovering you back to Himself again. Before you even were born and sinned, God al-

ready had the work deeded out from before the beginning of the creation to save sinners.

> *Behold, I will gather them out of all countries, whither I have driven them in mine anger, and in my fury, and in great wrath; and I will bring them again unto this place, and I will cause them to dwell safely: And they shall be my people, and I will be their God: Jeremiah 32:37-38*

> *And I said unto him, Sir, thou knowest. And he said to me, These are they which came out of great tribulation, and have washed their robes, and made them white in the blood of the Lamb. Therefore are they before the throne of God, and serve him day and night in his Temple: and he that sitteth on the throne shall dwell among them. They shall hunger no more, neither thirst any more; neither shall the sun light on them, nor any heat. For the Lamb which is in the midst of the throne shall feed them, and shall lead them unto living fountains of waters: and God shall wipe away all tears from their eyes. Revelation 7:14-17*

From the trouble of life under the hand of the enemy, these people are the redeemed – back in the hand of God once again!

> *Thou wilt shew me the path of life: in thy presence is fulness of joy; at thy right hand there are pleasures for evermore. Psalm 16:11*

God was not going to show us the path of Life before the time came to deal with that problem, while the enemy had hold of us. In His right hand was a title deed. Pleasures forevermore existed in this title deed to the Garden of Eden.

When Jeremiah doubted and explained the situation of the enemy in his prayer to God, his Lord told Him that nothing was too hard for Him. We need to know that God accomplished the necessary work to save us. Nobody was worthy to go in and take the book except the Lamb of God, Jesus Christ, God in the flesh. You were not saved by works, child of God. Nothing you can do could ever save you. It was far beyond your power. And for that reason, God came on the scene and did the work, Himself!

FIVE OTHER PICTURES IN REVELATION 5

When you stop and think about it, Revelation Chapter 5 consists of five pictures from the Old Testament.

One picture is the story in Jeremiah 32 and the sealed evidence.

Then there is the tradition of the Day of Atonement ritual, when the High Priest walked into the Holiest with blood of a sacrifice and obtained covering of sins for the entire nation of Israel.

There was the entrance back into the Garden of Eden to take a fruit of life, where in Revelation 10, Jesus tells John to take the book he unsealed and opened and to eat the Book.

Ezekiel 3 recorded God's words to Ezekiel telling him to eat a scroll and go forth and prophesy – (See Revelation 10).

JEREMIAH'S SEALED EVIDENCE

Moses went atop Mount Sinai and obtained the tablets of stone written on the front and on the backside – (Compare Exodus 32:15 with Revelation 5:1).

Noah's ark traversed the floodwaters to the mountain peak of Ararat (meaning "the Curse is reversed"), and obtained a covenant represented by a rainbow. John saw a rainbow about the throne.

Jesus walked into Heaven with His own blood, and washed our sins away, while at the same time obtained the title deed to the Garden of Eden, for the time had arrived to bring us back to God.

In His right hand were pleasures forevermore.

In 1 Peter 1:18-22, we read we were purchased back by the precious blood of Jesus. That is Revelation 5 all over again! Those who are purchased have believed the Gospel of God's work in raising Him from the grave. And these believers have obeyed the truth.

The deed has been stored in a safe place for 4,000 years from the time Adam sinned until Christ came. It sat in God's right hand, itself! Thank God He loved us so much that His vision shot across time to an appointed era in history in which He would see that deed opened once again!

16

DEATH AT THE ENTRANCE

And the LORD God said, Behold, the man is become as one of us, to know good and evil: and now, lest he put forth his hand, and take also of the tree of life, and eat, and live for ever: Therefore the LORD God sent him forth from the Garden of Eden, to till the ground from whence he was taken. So he drove out the man; and he placed at the east of the Garden of Eden Cherubims, and a flaming sword which turned every way, to keep the way of the tree of life. Genesis 3:22-24

...And they shall take of the blood, and strike it on the two side posts and on the upper door post of the houses, wherein they shall eat it. Exodus 12:7

The book of Genesis is simply packed full of abso-lutely precious gems of truth! Every detail holds within itself veritable storehouses of wealth. Consider again the thought of the Cherubims at the entrance of the Garden.

God said "Lest man should go to the tree of life and eat and live forever...." And then we read, "Therefore the Lord cast him out of the Garden of Eden."

DEATH AT THE ENTRANCE

A commonly misunderstood fact regards Adam's state of existence before the fall. We read in Romans 5 that death came as the result of sin. Therefore, since Adam had not sinned up until a certain time in his life, death was not a threat to him in the first stage of his existence.

> *Wherefore, as by one man sin entered into the world, and death by sin; and so death passed upon all men, for that all have sinned: Romans 5:12*

> *The soul that sinneth, it shall die. ... Ezekiel 18:20*

Death came only by sin. And there was a time when Adam simply had no sin!

Now that we know God's plan involved sending Christ to save us through death, we can see that God decided to seclude Adam away from the Garden's Tree of Life after Adam's sin. And what is unusual is that this was for the purpose of preserving Adam's potential to die after he sinned. God said man must be cast from the Garden so that he does not eat of the tree of Life and live forever.

EXCLUSION DUE TO MERCY

Was God being mean? Of course not! He acted in love. We noted earlier that God would save mankind through the death of Jesus Christ in vicarious atonement. Therefore, Adam had to continue to exist with the potential to die. If Christ's death was to be a vicarious death, it would have been ineffective in saving humanity who could not die. Christ would identify with Adam and his susceptibility to die through the death of the cross. Driving Adam away from the tree of life after his sin preserved the opportunity for Christ to die in Adam's stead.

Adam's death would cause him to return to the dust from which he was taken, and that was a necessity God had to preserve.

When God threw him out of the Garden, He placed a weapon of death at the entrance – a flaming sword. Had Adam attempted to re-enter the Garden, this sword, whirling in every direction, would have slain him instantly.

Notice that God originally took Adam from dust that existed outside the Garden and then brought the newly-created man into the Garden.

And the LORD God formed man of the dust of the ground, and breathed into his nostrils the breath of life; and man became a living soul. And the LORD God planted a Garden eastward in Eden; and there he put the man whom he had formed. Genesis 2:7-8

God did not take Adam from dust in the Garden's soil. Take note of what God told Adam...

In the sweat of thy face shalt thou eat bread, till thou return unto the ground; for out of it wast thou taken: for dust thou art, and unto dust shalt thou return. Genesis 3:19

GRAVES MUST BE OUTSIDE THE GARDEN

Adam would return to the dust from which he was made, and that meant he would be buried and would decay away in it. He would turn to dust again.

This Garden was a Holy Place. Recall the Holy of Holies in the Tabernacle and Temple was patterned after the Garden, with its only entrance on the east, also. We noted that the Cherubim blocking the Garden were depicted on a veil blocking man from getting into the holiest of holies. So the Garden was a Holiest of Holies. And sin is not allowed in there. (That is why Adam had to leave after he sinned.)

Since sin brings death, death was not allowed in the Garden. This means there were to be no graves in the Garden. Death could not enter that place.

So we see two things in view here:

Adam had to be preserved with the ability to die. (Had Adam eaten of the life fruit after he sinned, God said he would not die, so God took him out of there).

And Death could not get inside the Garden.

These two pictures have everything to do with New Testament salvation and they are brought to the forefront again, before Jesus came, in the story of the Exodus!

191

TAKE A BITE OF ETERNAL LIFE

DEATH, THE KEY TO SALVATION

The death penalty for sin was the very loophole intended to save mankind. God had to allow man to be able to die after he sinned so He could save man through death. One plan, and one plan alone, would work. If Adam could be rendered unable to die, having also sinned, then God would never be able to help him. So, He threw Adam from the Garden to keep him from eating fruit of life that he might live forever.

Get the picture:

God wanted man back. God wanted man in the Garden. Man was sinful and anything sinful that would try to enter the Garden would be killed by the flaming sword. So, how could God get sinful man back into a Garden when there stood a sword that would kill sinful men if they tried to enter?

Exodus shows a hint of the answer!

HINT OF MAN'S SALVATION IN THE EXODUS

Egypt was in complete upheaval because of a God who showed His stand for a people that were persecuted and en-slaved by a mad Pharaoh. Plagues struck that kingdom for days on end. Pharaoh turned into an insane man of fury and refused to let Israel go, while God hit him again and again with warnings in the form of those plagues. Finally, what God warned Pharaoh about before any plague ever began came to pass.

DEATH AT THE ENTRANCE

And thou shalt say unto Pharaoh, Thus saith the LORD, Israel is my son, even my firstborn: And I say unto thee, Let my son go, that he may serve me: and if thou refuse to let him go, behold, I will slay thy son, even thy firstborn. Exodus 4:22-23

Notice that warning was given as far back in the story as Chapter 4 of Exodus. However, before God fulfilled that threat, He sent plagues to try to change Pharaoh's mind. In Exodus Chapter 7, God began the plagues. Pharaoh refused to buckle under, and God did what He said he would do in the beginning. He slew the firstborn of every household in Egypt.

DEATH AT THE ENTRANCE

Get the picture. All firstborn children would die. But He told Israel to take a lamb that was spotless and kill it. They were to take its blood and put it specifically on the entrance of their homes, and stay inside the home until morning. When death was to come by, it would not be able to enter past that entrance. The Blood of the lamb would indicate to this slaying force that a death already occurred there! Death had already been paid at that home. There had already been a death at the entrance.

Blood was all around the entrances to the Israelites' homes. There was a *death at the entrance*. The act of an additional death was not permissible. As in the story of Genesis, death could not enter the Garden! Death's jurisdiction is limited to the domain outside the Garden. Death can go anywhere it pleases, except to one place, and one place only. Death could not enter the Garden. Graves would only be found outside the Garden. God sent Adam out to one day die in the dust outside the Garden from which he was originally made, but beyond the Garden entrance was eternal life. There stood the tree of life with fruit providing eternal life to the eater.

As we picture the story of Exodus as a *microcosm,* teaching us how all mankind can be saved by the blood of Jesus Christ, let us personify death for a moment. Imagine death's response to the state of the safety of humanity beyond the blood-stained doorway of Jesus Christ.

Death accuses God of unrighteousness in breaking His own rules. Death rages at how sinful man, rendered sinful since man's father Adam sinned, could be in a place where death cannot enter, for sinners must die! The soul that sins must die! How can sinful man enter into a place wherein death cannot reach him? So long as man has sinned, death has a right to stalk him his entire life, for the soul that sins shall die. Why is man beyond death's reach?

And mankind might protest as well in ignorance of God's wisdom. Man might cry out about inability to enter the Garden. The Garden had a flaming sword that blocked sinful man on the outside, for those who were able to die would indeed surely die upon entering the Garden with a flaming sword at its entrance. How can sinful man pass a barrier that slays sinful men from entering, let alone an entrance that prevents death from entering?

The answer for both dilemmas is the same.

DEATH AT THE ENTRANCE

"See the flaming sword at the entrance, death? Any who might try to enter past, with sin, will experience death at the entrance. Right there, no closer than the doorway, will they die. See that blood around the doors of the Hebrews in Egypt, Death?"

Think of it – there was indication of a death at the entrance! Just as in the Garden's entrance, should a sinner have attempted to pass, death would surely ensue.

And why is the one who sinned inside the house alive, anyway? Was it this living one's blood around the door, if that bloodshed stands for that one's death?

"Here is the Gospel, death. That blood came from the one who did not sin. A sinless and spotless lamb shed it. That lamb gave its life to pay the death penalty for the sinful for the sinful one. There must be a death for every sinful soul. *But nobody said another could not die in the place of the sinful one, so that the sinful one no longer was bound to pay the price.* That would enable to sinful one to be redeemed and enter once again into the original paradise in which God created him to dwell!"

All around the Kingdom of Egypt, the firstborn children of the Egyptians were slain that night. But none of the Israelite's children were slain, for a Lamb died in each of their places.

JESUS, THE LAMB TO BE SLAIN AT THE ENTRANCE

The next day John seeth Jesus coming unto him, and saith, Behold the Lamb of God, which taketh away the sin of the world. John 1:29

John called Jesus the Lamb of God who takes away the sin of the world. That room of every Hebrew home in Egypt, behind the blood, represented the Garden of God. Death could not enter there. We were sinful, but can now dwell in a sinless Garden because Jesus died for us. The only thing that barred us out was our sins. And death pays for sins. Jesus, therefore, took advantage of that rule and died for us, so we could enter.

See the lamb's blood on the door? See the sword at the door of the Garden? See the once sinful soul inside? Put the two pictures together, and realize that the Lamb, Jesus, took the death we would have experienced had we tried to enter. That blood indicated that the ones inside entered because another sinless one died as them. Death only needs to be paid once for every sinner.

There's been a death at the entrance!

Jesus can say "You would have died at the entrance, but I died there for you!"

The blood at the doorway represented Jesus, who took the death we would have taken had we tried to enter the Garden on our own. He did this so that we could indeed enter. Everyone who would attempt to enter would have experienced death. Since Christ's death stood for everyone's death, we can claim entrance and remain alive and free from the fear of death forevermore, having paid the death debt already.

ENTERING THE MOST HOLY PLACE, CANAAN

I had an interesting experience one night. While sleeping, I dreamed that I was preaching to our congregation. I preached about entering the land of Canaan, and how the Israelites doubted God's Word about their entrance.. In that dream, I recalled the picture of the holy of holies. I then distinctly correlated the idea of entering the Promised Land with entering the Most Holy place, and said in my dream, "We need a high priest so we can enter the holiest." That dream spoke volumes to me about the plan of God. I believe God inspired it. Scriptures came together in my mind the next day after I awoke.

The high priest could only enter the holiest if he had blood that represented the fact that a death had occurred, for blood in the body is the body's life, and blood shed from the body indicates the body's death. He had to walk past the veil embroidered with the likeness of the same creatures that stood by the sword in the Garden, because death would occur by the Cherubims should anyone enter.

Picture the High Priest approaching the Garden entrance, for that is what the Holy of Holies represented. There at the entrance, stood the force of death in the form of a flaming sword. In order for the High Priest to enter, death had to be informed that there was already a death. This principle applied to us when we first obeyed the Gospel and returned into this Garden paradise of fellowship with God's very presence.

"Let this man pass! Death, do you see the blood in his hand? He is showing you that death was already paid for him."

Now, my own personal blood would have been shed at the entrance had I tried to enter the Garden. But the blood was right there at the entrance in place where normally my blood would have been shed. So I am able to pass the entrance and not die, for a death already occurred there!

Unless you believe that Jesus died in your place, and you actually trust it to the extent that you fully believe you can go to Heaven and not die for eternity due to that blood of Jesus alone, you are lost. Unless you believe this so strongly that you will begin to live a life in obedience to everything the Bible says to live by, you will die in your sins.

Let us look at this issue of the sword at the entrance a little further.

17

GLORY RETURNS TO THE TEMPLE

*And he spake unto the man clothed with linen, and said,
Go in between the wheels, even under the cherub, and fill
thine hand with coals of fire from between the Cherubims,
and scatter them over the city. And he went in my sight.
Now the Cherubims stood on the right side of the house,
when the man went in; and the cloud filled the inner court.
Then the glory of the LORD went up from the cherub,
and stood over the threshold of the house; and the house
was filled with the cloud, and the court was full of the
brightness of the LORD'S glory. Ezekiel 10:2-4*

The return to the Garden is such a vital thought in
God's Plan that it is little wonder we find so many
allusions to that thought in as many Bible stories.
This tells us something. God has not been outdone by the
devil when the devil succeeded to tempt and defeat mankind
in the Garden so long ago. God did not have to resort to a
Plan B, and try something completely different. No. God set
out to continue to see His original intention for mankind fulfilled, albeit through the last man Adam, who is Jesus Christ.

LEAVING THE TEMPLE

After reading the above passage from Ezekiel's writings, the text continues to read about a cherub who was commanded to remove a coal of fire from between the other Cherubims on the chariot. Then we read of the cherub doing so, followed by the next bit of information.

> *Then the glory of the LORD departed from off the threshold of the house, and stood over the Cherubims. And the Cherubims lifted up their wings, and mounted up from the earth in my sight: when they went out, the wheels also were beside them, and every one stood at the door of the east gate of the LORD'S house; and the glory of the God of Israel was over them above. Ezekiel 10:18-19*

Then there are words of rebuke regarding men who devise mischief in the City, followed by this note:

> *Then did the Cherubims lift up their wings, and the wheels beside them; and the glory of the God of Israel was over them above. And the glory of the LORD went up from the midst of the city, and stood upon the mountain which is on the east side of the city. Ezekiel 11:22-23*

BACK TO THE TEMPLE AT THE POINT OF DEPARTURE

A similar picture is seen in the 43rd Chapter where the glory of God came from the East, sounding like many waters. It then entered into the Temple through the eastern entrance and filled the house. God then spoke to Ezekiel from within the house and said, "Son of man, the place of my throne, and the place of the soles of my feet, where I will dwell in the midst of the children of Israel for ever, and my holy name, shall the house of Israel no more defile, neither they, nor their kings, by their whoredom, nor by the carcases of their kings in their high places."

This is a tremendous sequence of events! The glory of God left the Temple from its eastern entrance, and later returned to the Temple and filled it again. Then God said this Temple will not be defiled again!

And finally, in the 44th Chapter of Ezekiel, God took Ezekiel to go to the eastern gate again, and Ezekiel saw that it was shut! God told him that it would remain shut because God entered the Temple by that gate, and it is reserved for the Prince. Only the prince shall enter that Gate and sit in the Temple and eat bread before the Lord. (Ezekiel 44:1-3).

EASTERN GATE, GOD'S GLORY AND SIN

All these references to the glory of God entering and exiting through the eastern Gate shed forth much insight into the overall plan of God which involves mankind. That glory was seen in the first part of Ezekiel as a Man seated on a throne, beneath Whom was a chariot which had four Cherubims at each of the four corners of the chariot. In the course of reading Ezekiel, we see a picture of the glory lifted from the chariot after which it entered the Temple through its east gate, and returned to the chariot after leaving the Temple.

The eastern gate, to say the least, definitely plays an important role in this writing of Ezekiel!

201

Also, in two separate instances, the cherubim actually stood at the eastern gate threshold (Ezekiel 10:2-3, 18-19).

These are the nothing less than the Cherubims first mentioned in the eastward entrance of the Garden of Eden after Adam's expulsion from paradise (Genesis 3:24).

In the book of Genesis, as in the book of Ezekiel, we read of an eastern gate, so to speak, where the cherubim stood, just as they stood at the east gate of the Temple when God's glory left the Temple. From this correlation of pictures we can begin to formulate the picture God obviously related to us throughout the entirety of the Bible. It is a message from the Lord regarding man and salvation.

To fully understand the picture, we must realize that salvation is required by man due to the great transgression of Adam and Eve when they disobeyed God in the Garden. For this reason they were cast out of the Garden, and were exiled to live outside of paradise where the tree of eternal Life stood. All Adam's children were born outside the Garden and were not allowed to enter there again, either. Since Adam sinned, and his children did not, many would think that the children should not be punished for their father's sake. However, we see that God did indeed bar them, too, from entering the Garden.

And we later read that Cain slew his brother, Abel, in jealousy after Abel's offering was accepted by God when Cain's was not. Why did Cain have that kind of hatred within him? Why did he sin? Where did such a nature come from? Adam did not portray any traits of self-centredness until after he ate of the forbidden fruit, when confronted by God. The answer to this involves the same reason Cain and Abel could not enter the Garden. They must have been born in sin.

The only explanation for the barring out of Cain and Abel, and the reason for Cain's sinful jealousy and murder, is that Adam's children were born with sin in their flesh which they inherited from their father. Paul pointed out this sin is also within all of us. We are born in a state of being banned from the Garden due to sin within the flesh of each of us.

> *Wherefore, as by one man sin entered into the world, and death by sin; and so death passed upon all men, for that all have sinned: Romans 5:12*

> *For as by one man's disobedience many were made sinners, so by the obedience of one shall many be made righteous. Romans 5:19*

MAN, THE GLORY OF GOD

Now, the element of the scenario that really makes the picture exciting is to notice that, just as God's glory left the Temple of Ezekiel's vision through the eastern gate, man left the Garden through the east gate! And man is referred to as the image and *the glory of God!*

> *For a man indeed ought not to cover his head, forasmuch as he is the image and glory of God: but the woman is the glory of the man. 1 Corinthians 11:7*

Paul said that man is the image and glory of God. In other words, the glory of God left the Temple/Garden through the east gate, as Cherubim stood at the threshold of the gate, when Adam left the Garden. This was exactly the manner in which God's glory left the east gate of the Temple when Cherubim stood there, too!

(Notice the idea of covering in 1 Corinthians 11 when we read about man and woman and the glory of God. Think about how the Cherubims were *covering* creatures, or keeping/protecting creatures, denoting guardianship and vigils of protection. See Ezekiel 28:16 and Genesis 3:24.)

When man left the Garden, we see a picture of God's glory leaving the Garden. And since the Garden had a single entrance in the east, and God's glory left Ezekiel's Temple through the east, we see another parallel thought. In noticing this, we also realize that God's glory must return to the Garden by way of having mankind return there in order to reinstate the perfect will of God for man.

GLORY LEFT SHILOH

The picture of God's glory leaving the Garden is again repeated in another story of the Bible, giving us indication that the message He is trying to get across to us about this issue is a very vital one indeed. He repeated the picture! After all, what could be more important than seeing man return to that place in which God first intended him to dwell?

> *And the whole congregation of the children of Israel assembled together at Shiloh, and set up the Tabernacle of the congregation there. And the land was subdued before them. Joshua 18:1*

GLORY RETURNS TO THE TEMPLE

After entering Canaan, the people set up the Tabernacle of God in Shiloh. In that Tabernacle would sit the Ark of the Covenant, where God's glory dwelt as first commanded in Exodus.

> *And thou shalt put the mercy seat above upon the ark; and in the ark thou shalt put the testimony that I shall give thee. And there I will meet with thee, and I will commune with thee from above the mercy seat, from between the two Cherubims which are upon the ark of the testimony, of all things which I will give thee in commandment unto the children of Israel.*
> *Exodus 25:21-22*

God spoke to His people from between the Cherubim on this ark.

The Tabernacle abode at Shiloh for over a century! In Samuel's time, the Tabernacle was still there. Generations later, two priests ministered to the Lord in Shiloh, Hophni and Phinehas, the sons of the high priest of the time, named Eli (1 Samuel 1:3)

These two sons were lewd fellows and committed of adultery with women who approached the Tabernacle. God revealed this to Samuel as a child, who was brought there to serve the priests in the Tabernacle. Samuel first began hearing God's voice while at Shiloh (1 Samuel 3:21).

In the passing of time, the day arrived when the Israelites battled the Philistines, and the two priests were sent to fetch the ark to the battle that they might not lose the war that began to favour the Philistines. They most likely recalled the time of the ark's march around Jericho when it brought down the walls of the city (1 Samuel 4:3).

However, Israel lost the battle that day and the Lord would not fight for them, obviously due to the sin of the priests. The Philistines took the ark, Hophni and Phinehas were killed, and their father Eli died when he heard the ark was taken from Israel. Phinehas' wife was pregnant at the time and near to giving birth to her baby when she heard that the ark was taken and her husband and Eli were killed. When she specifically heard that the Ark of the Covenant was taken from Israel, she named her child Ichabod, saying, "The glory is departed from Israel." (1 Samuel 4:19-22). She called the Ark of the Covenant by the title "the Glory of God".

THE GLORY IS DEPARTED. Just as the glory left the Garden and the Temple of Ezekiel, it left Shiloh that day due to the people's sin.

Jeremiah made mention of this event and commented, under inspiration of God, about the sin of Israel there.

> *But go ye now unto my place which was in Shiloh, where I set my name at the first, and see what I did to it for the wickedness of my people Israel. Jeremiah 7:12*

Much later, in David's time as king, the Ark was returned to Jerusalem from the Philistines. Israel accepted the presence of God and David erected a temporal Tabernacle for it. Later, when the Temple was built in Solomon's time, the ark was transported into this new structure as God's glory filled the Temple. In time, though, Israel's sin brought God's wrath down upon them again in the form of the Babylonian captivity. The Temple was smashed and the Ark was never seen since. God's glory had departed for the last time!

JESUS CHRIST: SHILOH, THE IMAGE, THE GLORY OF GOD AND THE LAST ADAM

Interestingly enough, a prophecy of Christ's coming was given in Genesis, and it mentioned a note about Shiloh.

> *The sceptre shall not depart from Judah, nor a lawgiver from between his feet, until Shiloh come; and unto him shall the gathering of the people be. Genesis 49:10*

Jesus was referred to as Shiloh, the same name that was given to the first location in which the Tabernacle was situated at Canaan! The word literally means "tranquil". (Could it refer to the peace in the paradise that was in the Garden, of which Shiloh's Tabernacle was a model?) Over a century the Ark remained in Shiloh until the sons of Eli removed it and lost it to the Philistines, as the Garden lost man, God's glory, due to man's sin.

The thought of Jesus being Shiloh, where the glory of God was meant to dwell, is coupled with the thought of Jesus being the last man Adam. Adam, remember, left the Garden as God's glory. And the ark left Shiloh, too. So, when we see Jesus regarded as both Shiloh and the last man Adam, we see a correlation to this great overall message!

> *And so it is written, The first man Adam was made a living soul; the last Adam was made a quickening spirit. 1 Corinthians 15:45*

TAKE A BITE OF ETERNAL LIFE

Nevertheless death reigned from Adam to Moses, even over them that had not sinned after the similitude of Adam's transgression, who is the figure of him that was to come. Romans 5:14

Adam was the figure of Jesus, Who would later come long after Adam's time.

Another connecting thought that seems to put the picture in even clearer view is the idea that John and Paul called Jesus the "glory" of God.

This beginning of miracles did Jesus in Cana of Galilee, and manifested forth his glory; and his disciples believed on him. John 2:11

When Jesus heard that, he said, This sickness is not unto death, but for the glory of God, that the Son of God might be glorified thereby. John 11:4

To God only wise, be glory through Jesus Christ for ever. Amen. Romans 16:27

For God, who commanded the light to shine out of darkness, hath shined in our hearts, to give the light of the knowledge of the glory of God in the face of Jesus Christ. 2 Corinthians 4:6

Jesus Christ is the glory of God. He is the image of God and the glory of God.

Who is the image of the invisible God, the firstborn of every creature: Colossians 1:15

He is the last Adam. Since Adam failed, God, Himself, became a man, and actually entered into the Temple!

We read Jesus cast out the moneychangers and upset their tables in the Temple. He cried that God's house was not to be a den of thieves, but rather a house of prayer (Luke 19:41-46)! The religious leaders had just rejected Jesus as He rode into Jerusalem, and would not recognize Him as the glory of God (Luke 19:38).

They rejected the return of God's glory! And He prophesied that the Temple would be destroyed without leaving one stone left upon another. It was as though the Babylonian captivity was repeated all over again! Forty years later to the very day, Rome came and besieged the City and destroyed the Temple, just as Jesus had predicted. And all this because they rejected the glory of God!

THE DOOR WAS SHUT

In Ezekiel's vision regarding the glory and the east gate, the east gate was to be shut and only opened for the prince, who could come in and eat bread before God. This is very similar to the picture of the Garden when the east gate was closed up by the presence of cherubim and a flaming sword. Adam could not enter the Garden, due to his sin, and eat of the tree of life and live forever. According to Ezekiel, only the prince could enter.

This fully agrees with the truth about Jesus Christ. He did not sin, and could, therefore, enter any holiest domain He wished to enter. He alone could enter such a domain, but He came that we, also, might return there! God's glory is meant to be in the Temple/Garden! Jesus came to open the way!

THE EAST GATE OPENED ONCE AGAIN

Jesus died on the cross and a marvelous thing happened! The veil in the Temple was ripped wide open, revealing the interior of the formerly secret most holy place (Matthew 27:50-53).

His death caused the veil to rip wide open in the Temple! The doorway that had been blockaded by the cherubim and the flaming sword, was now opened. Recall that the veil had images of cherubim sewn into it (2 Chronicles 3:14 *And he made the veil of blue, and purple, and crimson, and fine linen, and wrought Cherubims thereon.*)! This was identical to the picture seen of cherubim standing at the east threshold of the Temple when the glory of God left the structure.

What did this mean? Surely it had something to do with Christ's death being reason for the glory of God to enter the Temple again by way of the newly opened eastern gate! The veil blocked the single way into the Holiest of holies, and that entry faced east! Man, who was God's glory, was outside the Garden – outside the Temple – outside the place where he belonged. And Jesus did something about it!

You see, as the Ark of the Covenant, where God's glory dwelt, opened the barrier of the Jordan river that Israel might pass westward into Canaan (Joshua 3:15-16). Similarly, Jesus opened up the veil that man might enter the Temple again!

THE TRUE TEMPLE OF GOD

However, God does not truly dwell in Temples made by hands. Man would not enter the actual Temple of Herod in Jerusalem. Even Solomon knew that God dwells not in Temples made by man when he built the Temple. But God's name was to be represented by the Temple, and He chose Jerusalem to bear His name, or in other words, to be the location of the Temple. We must observe the picture of the Temple in Jerusalem to understand the work of the cross and what it accomplished.

Jesus Christ seemed to portray a dual role in the scene. He was indeed Adam's counterpart for the new creation, but He was also called Shiloh. Shiloh was the place where the Tabernacle stood in Canaan. Canaan may be referred to as counterpart to Eden, while Shiloh was the Garden that stood eastward within Eden. Mankind is reconciled to God by, as it were, entering the Body of Christ, for that is where God dwelt.

The literary structure of the following passage reveals that God was inside Christ, desirous of reconciling man to Him in that "location".

> For *it pleased the Father that in him should all fulness dwell; And, having made peace through the blood of his cross, by him to reconcile all things unto himself; by him, I say, whether they be things in earth, or things in heaven. And you, that were sometime alienated and enemies in your mind by wicked works, yet now hath he reconciled In the body of his flesh through death, to present you holy and*

211

unblameable and unreproveable in his sight:
Colossians 1:19-22

It was a picture of man returning to Shiloh, as God's glory, and once again entering the holiest of holies. And this picture, in turn, prefigured the return of man into Eden and the Garden in Eden.

The name "Jesus" actually interprets into English as "Jehovah our Salvation". God became manifest in flesh, and that flesh, therefore, was like a Tabernacle! This was the very thing He said when commenting that destruction of the Temple would move him to raise it again in three days. That was a reference to His body (John 2:19-21).

So we see that Jesus is the *Last Adam* that heads up the new creation, and also is the Tabernacle into which man, God's glory, must return. And that is the reason we read so much of the phrase "in Christ" throughout the New Testament. God's name, itself, was given to that Son of God who was that humanity in which God was manifested.

And unto his son will I give one tribe, that David my
servant may have a light alway before me in Jerusalem, the
city which I have chosen me to put my name there.
1 Kings 11:36

Israel later defiled the Temple, which actually meant they defiled God's "name".

But they set their abominations in the house, which is
called by my name, to defile it. Jeremiah 32:34

212

GLORY RETURNS TO THE TEMPLE

And, going back to Ezekiel, God showed His glory leaving the Temple and spoke about how Israel had defiled His Name.

> *In their setting of their threshold by my thresholds, and their post by my posts, and the wall between me and them, they have even defiled my holy name by their abominations that they have committed: wherefore I have consumed them in mine anger. Ezekiel 43:8*

These passages prove that the Temple represented God's name.

After the Gentiles received Spirit-filling in Acts 10, and we read of that event as follows:

> *And they of the circumcision which believed were astonished, as many as came with Peter, because that on the Gentiles also was poured out the gift of the Holy Ghost. For they heard them speak with tongues, and magnify God. Then answered Peter, Acts 10:45-46*

Later, Peter described the event as follows:

> *Simeon hath declared how God at the first did visit the Gentiles, to take out of them a people for his name. Acts 15:14*

The Gentiles became representative of God's name – precisely what the Temple represented!

God's people belong in the Garden — in the Temple – but the Temple is not a building as we know it. God's People

213

must be in Christ, the Temple, there where they are truly representative of God's name. It is a place of salvation! When Jesus Christ died, and paid for our salvation with His blood, the way into the Temple's holiest place was opened as the veil ripped in two. The veil represented His flesh which served as our means into the Holiest, or His Tabernacle entrance.

Having therefore, brethren, boldness to enter into the holiest by the blood of Jesus, By a new and living way, which he hath consecrated for us, through the veil, that is to say, his flesh; Hebrews 10:19-20

And since He died for our salvation, to bring us reconciliation to God through His death (Colossians 1:19-21), and reconciliation with God is found within Christ, that experience of salvation in our lives is our entrance back into the Garden. Adam left God's fellowship and, in effect, became an enemy of God. Through Christ's death on the cross, we became reconciled to Him spiritually "through" Christ, and fit to enter the Garden!

Let us live righteously before God, and not allow ourselves to lose place in the Garden/Temple, as Adam did. And let us not sin and commit iniquity so as to cause God's glory, mankind, to leave this holiest place of all! What fellowship with God exists in the Garden of our salvation! Let us remain in Christ.

John wrote of our need of living a holy life in order to fellowship with God.

That which we have seen and heard declare we unto you, that ye also may have fellowship with us: and truly our fellowship is with the Father, and with his Son Jesus Christ. And these things write we unto you, that your joy may be full. This then is the message which we have heard of him, and declare unto you, that God is light, and in him is no darkness at all. If we say that we have fellowship with him, and walk in darkness, we lie, and do not the truth: But if we walk in the light, as he is in the light, we have fellowship one with another, and the blood of Jesus Christ his Son cleanseth us from all sin. If we say that we have no sin, we deceive ourselves, and the truth is not in us. If we confess our sins, he is faithful and just to forgive us our sins, and to cleanse us from all unrighteousness. If we say that we have not sinned, we make him a liar, and his word is not in us. 1 John 1:3-10

My little children, these things write I unto you, that ye sin not. And if any man sin, we have an advocate with the Father, Jesus Christ the righteous: 1 John 2:1

May we remain in fellowship with God in this paradise of true Christianity. Walking in the light with Jesus is walking in the Garden!

COMING IN 2007

FROM DUTY TO OPPORTUNITY

A new book by Jamen Nicholson

Ye cannot serve God and mammon.

The proper order is Mammon serving you, and you serving God.

When we put the god of mammon on its knees before the one true God, with the intention of being blessed so that we might bless the Kingdom and not ourselves, then God will bless us personally with true Spiritual riches!

This book details a biblical and systematic approach for spiritual, physical and financial prosperity in life. Results, not just preached, but experienced. Read about a young man who found himself down to the last $100 in his pocket, to making over $400,000, in four years – what it has accomplished in his home and family, in his own spiritual life to seeing the Kingdom of God blessed in the earth.

from Garden City Publications